Spank THE *Bank*

THE Guide to Alternative Business Financing

KARLENE SINCLAIR-ROBINSON

outskirtspress
DENVER, COLORADO

Spank The Bank
The Guide to Alternative Business Financing
All Rights Reserved.
Copyright © 2013 Karlene Sinclair-Robinson
Editor: Barry Cohen, AdLab Media Communications, LLC
Author's Cover Photo: Elza Daniel, Photographer, Elza Photography
v3.0

Outskirts Press, Inc.
http://www.outskirtspress.com

ISBN: 978-1-4327-9461-3

Library of Congress Control Number: 2012916592

Outskirts Press and the "OP" logo are trademarks belonging to Outskirts Press, Inc.

PRINTED IN THE UNITED STATES OF AMERICA

TABLE OF CONTENTS

SECTION 4

SECTION 5

ABOUT THE AUTHOR

FOREWORD

Every life you touch changes you. With every life that touches you, you change. We form connections; we build bridges; we humanize our surroundings with every interaction. As an author and editor of several books, I have personally interacted with and impacted many lives. With each author I helped, I also grew—and will continue to grow.

When Karlene Sinclair-Robinson came into my life, the synergies between us exploded. The relationship not only became symbiotic, it evolved almost instantly to become telepathic. Our thoughts merged. Karlene impacts lives weekly, daily and even hourly. As a business owner and consultant to fledgling businesses, she guides, nurtures, steers and sometimes chastises her clients onto the highway of growth. As an author, teacher and speaker, she continues to excite, stimulate and provoke action. When you read this book, you will find yourself in the moment with her. That is her gift.

Karlene will take you on a journey to the winner's circle—but only if you want it badly enough to follow her plan. Perhaps it stems from her experiences as a mother; perhaps, her insight into success grew out of her recognition of her own failures; perhaps her burning, bursting desire to succeed, coupled with her willingness to *share* her success, led her to a place where she could extend her willing hand to others. With all of the above, the one element never missing from any aspect of Karlene's life that surely propelled her to write this book was her *faith*.

Every day each of us will face challenges and tests. Place your faith in Karlene as you walk through the pages of this book. She will lead the way. Dare to follow her, as many have, and you will reach your potential. Whether you are just now contemplating starting a business, in the process of launching your enterprise or struggling to grow your existing business, *Spank the Bank* will provide you with the critical insights and proven strategy to get there.

Barry Cohen
Author, *10 Ways to Screw Up an Ad Campaign*
Co-author, *Startup Smarts*
Co-author, *Comin' Home*

Special Thanks

To:

Melinda Emerson

Author of Be Your Own Boss in 12 Months

&

Carol Roth

Author of The Entrepreneur Equation

ACKNOWLEDGMENTS

To the following individuals, in no particular order, I say "Thank You" for your support, prayers and encouragement:

- Barry Cohen, Editor/Consultant, AdLab Media Communications

- Kevin Clark, 'Mr. Big Mortgage', Clark Capital Group

- Pauline Leitch, Director, Women's Business Center, Community Business Partnership – Springfield, VA

- Staff of the Community Business Partnership – Springfield, VA

- Dannelle Shugard – Article Editor/ Social Media Expert

- Sally Shields – Bestselling Author

- Horace L. Robinson

- Deborah Rowe and Yanic Thomas – Inner Circle Partners

- Kathleen Manley, Asset Funding Solutions, Inc.

For those who are not named here, please know that you are thought of. You know who you are! Your imprint in both my personal and professional life is invaluable, and I will always cherish it. I sincerely thank you all.

I must give thanks to God, my heavenly father, for providing me with the wisdom and foresight to take my dream of being a valuable individual in society to a higher level. Without Him, none of this would have been possible.

When I need the strength to carry on, this where I go…

Psalm 121: 1-8 *(King James Version (KJV))*

¹ I will lift up mine eyes unto the hills, from whence cometh my help.

² My help cometh from the LORD, which made heaven and earth.

³ He will not suffer thy foot to be moved: he that keepeth thee will not slumber.

⁴ Behold, he that keepeth Israel shall neither slumber nor sleep.

⁵ The LORD is thy keeper: the LORD is thy shade upon thy right hand.

⁶ The sun shall not smite thee by day, nor the moon by night.

⁷ The LORD shall preserve thee from all evil: he shall preserve thy soul.

⁸ The LORD shall preserve thy going out and thy coming in from this time forth, and even for evermore.

Isaiah 41:10 *(King James Version (KJV)*

¹⁰ Fear thou not; for I am with thee: be not dismayed; for I am thy God: I will strengthen thee; yea, I will help thee; yea, I will uphold thee with the right hand of my righteousness.

Proverbs 3:5-6 *(King James Version (KJV)*

[5] Trust in the Lord with all thine heart; and lean not unto thine own understanding.

[6] In all thy ways acknowledge him, and he shall direct thy paths.

INTRODUCTION

Ten years ago, the thought of writing a book never entered my mind. Today, you are reading a more in-depth and newly published version of my first book. As a child, do you remember thinking of what you wanted to be when you grew up? I am sure you had many dreams and aspirations. You might have accomplished many of them already, while still planning to fulfill many more. Well, for me, I had only one thought. Growing up in Jamaica, I remember having only one wish. It was a prayer. It was this: I would ask God to let me live till I was 20, then I would not bother Him for anything else.

Interesting concept but then, that was the thinking of a child. As a child, I felt that if God just answered that one prayer, I would be forever grateful and not bug Him for more as he had already done enough. I felt that if He kept His word, then I would do so too; I would not ask Him for anything else.

When that prayer was answered, I made sure to keep my promise. For the next 17 years, I distinctly remember always being thankful for what I had. I was grateful for the job that was not so great, the friends that were not real friends, the parent that was not there, the teacher that did not understand, and through it all, being absolutely grateful for the life I had. I was grateful for the job, the parent that was there, the teachers who did understand, and for all the other blessings throughout my life.

This all changed four years ago, when something very powerful happened to me. I learned the true power of forgiveness. In learning this lesson, I realized I had a right to ask God for guidance in understanding my purpose and what I was called to do. I knew there was more to me than being one of many. I felt a strong sense that there was much more to me than what I could see. It felt as though something was missing and that I had to pay attention to the strong feeling within that there was much more.

I cannot say this came about from reading a book or listening to a particular person, minister, motivational speaker or otherwise. I can say this though; I looked within myself. I started asking God questions regarding what mission He was calling me to. We all have a mission to accomplish. I have finally recognized the mission I have been called to take on, and so, I say to you, are you ready for your mission? Your purpose? Do you even know what that mission is, or are you still struggling to find yourself?

Why did I share my story with you? Well, you do not know me. In order to help others in whatever capacity we can, we must give of ourselves. So, in giving of myself, I felt I should share this one very important part of me with the thought that if it can move one person in the right direction, I would have achieved what I set out to accomplish: fulfilling the mission I was called to.

You have a message to bring forth; look within, seek out the answers and they will appear. Before you can fully achieve your goals and the mission you are supposed to fulfill, you must learn and understand the following:

- **Courage** – You must have the courage to take your dreams from an idea to reality.

- **Action** – You must get up and do the things necessary that will bring you closer to making those dreams real.

- **Faith** – You must have faith in God, your skills and the belief that your dreams will come true. You cannot worry about things seen and unseen that could stop you in your tracks.

- **Perseverance** – You must have the strength to go the distance in working towards the creation of your dreams.

- **Gratitude** – You must be grateful for what you have today and continue doing so throughout your life.

- **Forgiveness** – You must forgive anyone that you feel has wronged you in whatever capacity they did so. Forgiveness is not about letting the other person off the hook for what they did or did not do; it is about releasing yourself to be able to reach your full potential.

Without them you will not take that idea, that business, or that relationship to the level of success you envision. Letting go of the baggage you have carried with you for so long is a must. Without a clean and clear picture of the mission you are to take on, you will be bogged down wondering why you cannot get the idea to become a reality, why your business is always on the brink of failure, or why your relationships always end up in the dumps.

Finally, the world needs you. Your ideas, your services or products are needed to make this world a better place. Do not worry about how much competition might be out there. There is always a niche you can carve out for yourself. Be sure though that what you do is for the benefit and good of those it can help.

Make sure it is not all about "Money". Making it just about how much money you can make will not take you to the heights of success you could achieve. Remember, those who made it only about money, did not stand the test of time. They ended up losing it all.

So, make it about the people you can help. When your products or services have helped enough people, your money will flow accordingly. Do good and it will follow you!

AUTHOR'S NOTE

Over the years, I have counseled many startups and seasoned business owners at various levels, and unfortunately, I see the same pattern. Start-ups are running scared not knowing where to go or how to get there, while waiting too long to seek assistance. It is the same for well-established businesses. These businesses are operating with poor balance sheets, negative cash flows and operating on the proverbial "robbing from Peter to pay Paul" mentality.

Then, there are those who are solely operating out of "Greed". This is creating so many felons, you read correctly, as more and more business owners are stealing from their businesses, families and others to make things work, or chasing after opportunities they should not be chasing. This is unfortunate.

The purpose of this book is to expand the reader's mind on how to take your business through the journey of survival or growth in today's tight lending arena. Having access to capital is vital to everyone. You are affected by negative cash flow and financing issues whether you are a startup or a business doing $20 million or more annually. Realizing the issues affecting you is important, while creating and executing on solutions that can keep you from financial ruin, is crucial.

This book is not about fighting with banking institutions or bringing them down. Maybe we do need to enact changes. In the meantime, banks are lending. Let me repeat. <u>BANKS ARE LENDING</u>. *You just cannot qualify for it.*

Those who can qualify for bank financing, great! It is the least expensive way to finance your business, so make good use of it. Either way, collaboration, or teamwork if you will, is one of the keys to getting this economy back on track. Lending institutions and private lenders working together to benefit those in need, is important.

We must stem the hemorrhage of businesses closing their doors due to a lack of capital. This is also due to a lack of knowledge. When entrepreneurs cannot qualify for bank loans, they need alternatives. We must adjust to the changing tide of market demands.

We must also continue to work together to make access to capital a vital opportunity for those who are honest, hardworking and still believe in the American Dream.

FINALLY...

This book is here to guide you through the maze of options that might be of benefit to your company. Using this resource will help to put you on the path to becoming more profitable. This is entirely up to you though. It will give you access to information that will help you figure out when you need to use one alternative financing option over another. You will be able to understand and use a variety of options that the banks do not advertise, will not or cannot offer.

I am committed to helping dedicated business owners through creative solutions that are legal and appropriate. So, whatever your situation, I want you to send me your stories after reading and putting to use the information this book provides. I would love your feedback and to be able share your stories, with your permission of course. I look forward to hearing from you. Email me via: Info@ SpankTheBank.biz

SECTION 1

"The Fear of Success is just as debilitating as the Fear of Failure. Do not let either one hold you back."

~Karlene Sinclair-Robinson

BUSINESS ESSENTIALS

The life of an entrepreneur is never an easy task. It takes tenacity, courage, faith and the attitude of never giving up in order to make it. Whether you are just starting out or have been in business for years, the path to entrepreneurial success is always a bumpy road to travel.

There is no straight line to success. You must travel the winding road on your journey to achieving the goals you have set. This is where what you know will help you and what you do not know could hurt you. Knowing the essentials of operating a business is vital. Understanding the requirements of being a business owner in your industry is critical to your success.

So, continue reading this book, one chapter at a time. Use the information provided to make you and your business better and greater.

Success to you!

CHAPTER 1

Who Needs Access To Capital?

Everyone! Most business owners today have some type of cash flow issue that warrants the need for a cash infusion. Whether there is a need to finance payroll, ramp up funding for that new contract, or covering the cost of a new purchase order, having "Access to Capital" is a vital necessity in any economy.

Walking into the local branch of your bank and getting a loan just like that is a thing of the past. You know it. That's why you are reading *"SPANK THE BANK"*. You have been there or you know someone who has.

Have you tried getting a loan lately? What was your experience? Did you qualify for the financing or not? How many banks did you have to pass through before finally succeeding? Were you able to secure the financing? Did you get the original amount you were seeking? Did you have to pledge more collateral than you expected?

So many questions, yet the answers might not be as clear. Why? Where do you go when the source you are accustomed to using for your financial needs is no longer operating as they did a few years ago? When your bank has turned you down, whom do you turn to for help? Another bank? The SBA? Who?

All the questions in the previous paragraphs lead directly to the dilemma faced by so many fledgling entrepreneurs today. These are all questions many of you have asked yourself and have come up short on the answers. Your answers to those questions and more

I

tell the story of what many face on a day to day basis. Those who are seeking and keep reaching for that dream of entrepreneurial success must take a long hard look at the reality of these issues.

We have seen what can happen when entrepreneurs are not able to access the money needed for "Growth" or "Survival". We end up with so many businesses closing. This is why there are so many commercial properties with "Vacant" signs. So many businesses have closed their doors all across this country, and still there is no end in sight to this dilemma.

As you read on, I will be addressing the issues facing startups and eager entrepreneurs wanting to understand and succeed in this tight financial market by providing possible solutions for you. I realize many individuals who are now startups, were prior business owners who failed in their previous endeavors but are still determined to make it happen; while others have been around the block but struggling with the current tide of limited borrowing power.

Where Are You?

In the last few years, going back to the start of the financial meltdown in 2008 many businesses were laying off large numbers of employees and even closing their doors. It is still happening today, what with the low job numbers reported, and businesses having to decide on drastic measures just to survive.

Is this what the American dream was about? Certainly not! With the economic downturn, many are wondering what they can or cannot do to stay afloat. What about starting your own business or keeping your business open? Is it the right time for you to do so? How do you survive in this financially strapped mine-field?

The answers depend on your situation and the research you do. Businesses can start during a recession and still succeed. Both General Electric® and Microsoft®, two of the most successful businesses in history, did just that.

This financing guide is a resource for those individuals who are determined to succeed, whether you just got started or have been struggling under the weight and pressure of limited cash flow. This book will provide some guidance or a refresher on alternative ways to finance your business's funding needs. It is about getting creative when times get tough.

Maybe you have been struggling with your business for a few years. You might have been turned down for a small business loan by your bank. Maybe you have been somewhat successful but have not really looked into financing options to move your business to the next level. These are all things to think about, then choose a path to success. Let us transition to the next level by taking the action steps necessary in order to achieve a level of success that astounds us.

STARTING OUT

So you want to start your own business. Great idea! But is it? Have you done your research and crunched your numbers, and is it still making sense? After your number crunching, did you finally figure out how much you actually need to get started? Do you have the amount needed to get started? If not, where do you plan to get it-- from family or friends, or from the bank? What about your business plan? Do you need training? Do you need personnel to get the business off the ground or is this a one-man (or woman) show? Have you considered incorporating versus going sole proprietorship? Do you plan to open a commercial space or work from home?

So many questions to consider! Venturing into the business world is not to be taken lightly. The answers to these questions are vital in helping you determine exactly how you need to proceed. Once you have figured out what you want to do, then you should seek out the necessary assistance to help you succeed.

3

STAYING THE COURSE

If you have been in business but have been struggling, have you stopped to review your business plan lately? Oh, by the way, did you actually write one? Did you just admit to not writing one? What are you waiting for? Do you know the reason for a business plan? No? Well, guess what. It is your business road map. This plan helps guide you through the next one to five years, or however long you choose to plan for.

Remember, it is a plan for the future, not a report of what you have already done. Without this plan, you will not succeed to your fullest potential. Even if you have been doing fairly well, if you had written the plan, you would have done a lot better, so get to writing it now! Here are a few resources to help you: www.BPlan.com, www.SBA.gov or www.SCORE.org.

Why do you think everywhere you go for financing, the first things they want are your executive summary and business plan? Think! These documents tell financiers what you plan to do, why you need their money and your strategy for paying back the loan. A business plan also shows them whether you know what you are talking about or not. You will not receive any type of monetary assistance outside of your family and friends without these documents, except for a couple of alternative options. Whether you are just starting out or have been around the block, you still need to have a plan.

After listening to the horror stories of some business owners, I knew I had to change the financial mindset of those of you who might otherwise make the same mistakes. This is the reason for this book, to help you know more about alternative financing, how to qualify for it, and how to use it like the big boys and girls.

THE CHALLENGES

The challenges and problems facing you in today's economy are like climbing Mount Everest. The banking sector cannot finance most small businesses. Why? Businesses with limited history, poor financial positions and poor leadership do not make good candidates for the banks to finance. Banks operate in a risk-averse manner.

Biz Tip:

Do not wait until the last minute to address your business financing needs. The solution will not be waiting for you. Be prepared.

With the turmoil affecting the banking sector and so many lending institutions, now more than ever is it truly difficult to get a loan without extremely good credit and solid historical data to back up your request. Banks can and will finance only companies with strong financial positions, great leadership and a solid plan that enables the bank to get great future returns on their investments with minimal risk exposure. Understanding this fact is critical; so do not beat your head against the wall when you are turned down.

An important piece to note about banks is that they look back at your past performance, both personal and business history if you have one, in order to define their risk exposure. If the banker feels the risk is too great, then you will be denied--but if they feel it is well within the level of what they look for, then it is a go. You must consider and understand banking institutions' aversion to risk before approaching them for a loan.

Seeking Alternative Financing

The current national (even global) financial situation, with all the changes in today's market, makes it even harder to qualify for bank financing. Balancing the scale in this arena is vital, but will it even out for you? This is where you have got to know what is available. Once you understand the value of a financial product that could work for your company, do not hesitate to make contact with the financing sources to discuss what is best for you from the various

Biz Tip:

"Procrastination" will stop you from achieving the SUCCESS you deserve. Fix this problem by taking action. Get to work today!

products available.

Ask questions and do not be afraid to investigate and learn how a particular financing option can help you and your business. It is vital for you to understand each option clearly before making a decision. Some options are great for now, while others will be better down the road. The key is, knowing what is available, what is coming down the line to help you in the future, and when you need to use a particular alternative financing solution.

Procrastination is a huge deterrent to success. If you are a procrastinator, do not blame others for your failings or for not getting that contract or new business. Similarly, knowing your plan and exercising all financing options available is critical to the success of your business. Putting things off is no excuse, especially when it could mean the survival of your business.

CHAPTER 2

Business Basics:
What Every Business Owner Should Know

This chapter covers some of the most essential aspects of being in business. It is not easy, as you know, to start a business or to stay in business for that matter. It takes up all your time, energy, and focus, and heaven help you if you have a family with young children. If this is you, do not be afraid! You will be okay, but only if you are serious about succeeding in your chosen business endeavor. Hopefully, you have the family support you need.

Starting a business can seem intimidating at times. For those who have already done so, it still might not be easy. Understanding and navigating through the maze of things to do as a business owner that works with the consumer, commercial or governmental markets can be a daunting process. Once you understand the basics, you can determine the best ways to grow your company and determine the avenues you want to pursue.

First, knowing what type of entity you want to create is important for a number of reasons. When you set up your business correctly, you do not leave yourself open to certain liabilities. This does not mean you are exempt if you do something illegal. If you do, you will pay the penalty. However, there are some protections you may want to avail yourself of when choosing the structure of your business.

1. To Incorporate or Not to Incorporate

Have you considered what legal structure to use for your company? If you have been in business as a "Sole Proprietor", you might want to seriously consider forming an entity. You can form a limited liability corporation (LLC), a subchapter "S" corporation (S-Corp), or a partnership, or maybe you decided to go for a sole proprietorship. Operating as a sole proprietor will affect your ability to access some forms of alternative financing.

The decision you made or make at this juncture is very critical from a financial and legal standpoint. Understanding each legal structure will help you decide what suits you best. Keep in mind that all legal formats carry some legal protection, except for operating as a sole proprietorship.

In many instances, being a sole proprietor can be a drawback when seeking financing. This type of business ownership can limit your access to financing, as all decisions are based on your personal financial strength. If you are running your business as a one-person business with no inclination of expanding and you are comfortable with where you are, that's great. If you are seeking to expand, take on new employees, larger jobs or contracts, it is vital that you choose a legal status comparable to your business needs.

In making this decision, be certain to seek out an attorney and a certified public accountant (CPA) who can give you sound advice from a legal or tax standpoint. It is important that you understand the reasons behind these legal structures and the ramifications of choosing one form over another. For example, creating a

Biz Tip:

Many funding sources will not work with you unless you have formally registered your company. They prefer that you not operate as a "Sole Proprietor".

8

limited liability company or corporation can better protect you by separating your business from your personal assets in the event of a civil suit.

For tax purposes, however, you should seek professional advice as to the best entity format that would fit your need. If you decide to create a limited liability company, you have limited tax liabilities. A Subchapter "S" Corporation may result in higher tax liability for you. A "C" corporation generally incurs the highest rate of taxation, and is the preferred form of organization if you plan to take your company public. Most important, you can change the form of organization at a later date if it becomes more advantageous—although there are often tax consequences. Get an attorney and a CPA on board as soon as possible.

2. EMPLOYER IDENTIFICATION NUMBER (EIN) AND TAX IDENTIFICATION NUMBER (TIN)

All current and newly created businesses must obtain an Employer Identification Number (EIN) or tax identification number, a number issued by the Internal Revenue Service to identify each entity. If you are operating as a sole proprietor, you will continue to use your Social Security number or you can apply for a tax ID number.

You will need to complete the IRS Form SS-4 (Application for Employer Identification Number) in order to apply for your EIN. The IRS provides numerous publications and other materials to better assist you. To obtain information, visit the IRS Web site. (See Web sites under the appendices.)

3. NAICS – YOUR INDUSTRY CODES

NAICS is the acronym for the North American Industry Classification System. It is the standard used by Government Agencies to classify businesses. These agencies use the data they collect, assess and publish in relation to the U.S. Business economy.

Be sure to check and know what your specific industry codes are. You can have multiple NAICS codes based on the goods and/or services you provide. You may access the NAICS online via their web site. (See Web sites under the appendices.)

4. CENTRAL CONTRACTOR REGISTRATION

If you plan to do business with the Federal, State, or Local government, you must register your company with the Central Contractor Registration (CCR). This site collects, verifies and stores data on all companies wanting to do business with the government in support of their acquisition requirements.

All prospective vendors must be registrants to the CCR before they can be awarded a contract, including blanket purchase order agreements, through certain government agencies. Information is located at the CCR Web site, www.CCR.gov.

5. DUN & BRADSTREET

All firms should have a Data Universal Numbering System number, which is assigned by Dun & Bradstreet. Dun & Bradstreet is the country's leading source of business credit information. It provides information on each business entity and enables lending institutions and others to make sound business and/or financial decisions involving your company. It helps these institutions, business associates and others mitigate any risk from being associated with you. Understanding how Dun & Bradstreet uses information provided to them about you and your company is critical to moving your business forward.

If you plan to do business with any local, state or federal government agency, you must obtain the number Dun & Bradstreet assigns your company. You can also use this number to monitor your own company's credit rating. You can also use its system, at a cost of course, in obtaining information on potential clients you might want to do business with. The information you receive on a company's credit worthiness and financial viability will also help you make sound client-related decisions.

To learn more about Dun & Bradstreet, visit its web site. See our Web site listings under the appendices at the end of this book.

6. SMALL OR MINORITY CERTIFICATION

Many businesses qualify to be classified as a certified minority company. To become a certified minority company, you have a number of qualifying factors to determine your company's status. Due to the vast list of industries and subgroups, it makes for an extensive list. Visit the SBA's web (http://www.SBA.gov) site to get the full list. Here are some of the basic qualifications:

SMALL BUSINESS CLASSIFICATION

- Privately owned

- Number of employees and income level

- Must be a for-profit organization

WBE	WOMEN BUSINESS ENTERPRISE
WOSB	WOMEN-OWNED SMALL BUSINESS
MBE	MINORITY BUSINESS ENTERPRISE
DBE	DISADVANTAGED BUSINESS ENTERPRISE
SDVOSB	SERVICE-DISABLED VETERAN-OWNED SMALL BUSINESS
HUBZONE	HISTORICALLY UNDERUTILIZED BUSINESS ZONES
8(A)	8(A) BUSINESS DEVELOPMENT PROGRAM

Check with your state minority certification department for further information.

7. BUSINESS LICENSE AND INSURANCE

In most counties and/or states throughout the United States, it is a requirement that you obtain a business license in order to operate within that local jurisdiction. You do not have to have business insurance to start your business. It is advisable though that you seek coverage, as your risk exposure is elevated without an insurance policy in place, in the event of a lawsuit. Depending on the type of business you have or want to start, you need to factor in business insurance as a high-priority expense. This includes liability coverage, property and casualty, and workers' compensation if you have employees. For certain professional service companies, professional liability insurance may also provide needed protection.

8. BANKING – PERSONAL VS. BUSINESS

It is often noted by CPAs, bookkeepers, bankers and other lenders accessing clients' or borrowers' financial documents that frequently discrepancies will come up. These discrepancies show up on the financial statements of both start-ups and seasoned businesses. This usually spells trouble for the business and the entrepreneur if they are ever audited by the Internal Revenue Service (IRS).

This may seem basic to some of you reading this, but it is important for others reading this book to know. Many individuals will say they did not know they could not pay their personal bills with the company's credit card or check. This is called "Co-Mingling" of funds. If you have been doing this or were considering it, please stop! Per the IRS you are not to mix your business income and your personal banking. When you earn money through your company, it must be paid to the company and deposited into the business checking account.

Your business checks and business ATM card must not be used to pay your personal expenses. They are for your business expenses only. So, be sure to define what these business expenses are. Use your Cash Flow Statement to help you keep track of what your business is doing.

For the legal ramifications of this and more, check with your Attorney, CPA and visit the IRS's website to learn more. Not only does this practice cause a bookkeeping, tax and accounting nightmare, it could also jeopardize the protection afforded to an incorporated business by allowing a plaintiff in a legal action against you to "pierce the corporate veil", making you personally liable and exposing your assets.

9. US CITIZEN AND IMMIGRATION SERVICE

The U.S. Citizenship and Immigration Services, through the Federal Immigration Reform and Control Act of 1986, requires all employers to verify the employment eligibility of all new employees. This law requires you, the employer, to process an Employment Eligibility Verification Form (I-9). The form documents an employee's work eligibility status in the United States. Each employee must present documentation that proves they are eligible for employment, such as a US passport, signed Social Security card, Permanent Resident Alien Card, Work Authorization document, or any other documentation listed on the USCIS Form I-9 Instruction sheet.

> **USCIS e-Verification System & Employment Eligibility Form (I-9)**

In order to comply with this process of hiring legal employees, all new workers must be checked through the USCIS E-Verification system via their website. It will ask for specific data from the IRS I-9 Form. Once you enter the correct information into their system, they will respond accordingly with their results. The information you receive must be stored with the person's I-9 Form.

This is a warning to those business owners and start-ups that believe they can bypass this process. The government is making sure that you comply with this law. They will impose strict fines against your company if you are found in violation of this Act. In fact, the amounts of these fines have actually forced some small businesses to close up shop. The fines could be as high as $10,000 per violation and can include jail time.

Biz Tip:

Verify ALL employees' work eligibility status through the USCIS E-Verification system. Be sure to keep accurate records in case your company comes up for investigation.

You may contact the Employer Hotline at **(800) 357-2099** to learn more, or to request forms, you can call **(800) 870-3676**. To learn more, please visit the U.S. Citizenship and Immigration Services website at: http://www.uscis.gov

10. Occupational Safety and Health Administration (OSHA)

All businesses are affected by the laws and guidelines set forth by the Occupational Safety and Health Administration (OSHA). These guidelines are especially important based on the type of business or industry you operate in. You are also governed by these guidelines if you hire employees. The labor law posters must be displayed at your business location(s).

One such guideline is the "Handwashing Policy". If you have ever been out to eat at a restaurant and had to use their restrooms, then I am sure you have seen such a sign. If not, start taking notice of where these signs are; even looking out for the fire extinguisher and sprinkler system in your grocery store. These all fall under the OSHA regulations in order to keep both employees and customers safe. You can learn more about these guidelines from OSHA's website at http://www.OSHA.gov or Department of Labor at:

http://www.dol.gov/oasam/programs/osdbu/sbrefa/poster/matrix.htm

11. LABOR LAWS GOVERNING EMPLOYERS

There are many laws governing a business with employees. Some Federal laws are applicable to your business based on the number of employees you have employed while other laws are for all business entities with staff. The Department of Labor is the department of the government that governs compliance with these laws.

The monetary penalties for not being compliant with these laws can range as high as $10,000 per employee and up to $11,000 per child labor violation. Please reference the list of applicable labor laws in the Appendices at the back of the book. Visit the Department of Labor's website at http://www.dol.gov.

12. NEW LAW – OFFICIAL SUMMARY

S. 181 (111th): Lilly Ledbetter Fair Pay Act of 2009

Lilly Ledbetter Fair Pay Act of 2009 - Amends the Civil Rights Act of 1964 to declare that an unlawful employment practice occurs when: (1) a discriminatory compensation decision or other practice is adopted; (2) an individual becomes subject to the decision or practice; or (3) an individual is affected by application of the decision or practice, including each time wages, benefits, or other compensation is paid. Allows liability to accrue, and allows an aggrieved person to obtain relief, including recovery of back pay, for up to two years preceding the filing of the charge, where the unlawful employment practices that have occurred during the charge filing period are similar or related to practices that occurred outside the time for filing a charge. Applies the preceding provisions to claims of compensation discrimination under the Americans with Disabilities Act of 1990 and the Rehabilitation Act of 1973.

Amends the Age Discrimination in Employment Act of 1967 to declare that an unlawful practice occurs when a discriminatory compensation decision or other practice is adopted, when a person becomes subject to the decision or other practice, or when a person is affected by the decision or practice, including each time wages, benefits, or other compensation is paid.

Source: http://www.govtrack.us/congress/bills/111/s181

13. FEDERAL MINIMUM WAGE - $7.25

It is important to note that the Federal guidelines governing wages, specifically the minimum amount employers can legally pay an employee is set currently at $7.25. Some states have a higher rate or lower rate, while others have no minimum wage. Reference the table below to see where your state minimum wage is set or visit the

Biz Tip:

It is a federal crime to pay your employees below the minimum wage and for not paying overtime where applicable. Check your state regulations for additional employer requirements.

U.S. Department of Labor website for more. There are only a few categories of employees that are exempt, such as restaurant waiters and waitresses and certain domestic workers. *Visit the following website to find your state's minimum wage amount: http://www. dol.gov/whd/minwage/america.htm*

14. RECORD KEEPING FOR SMALL BUSINESS

Did you know that there is an extensive list of records or documents that you must keep on hand for a period of time? Do you know what these documents are or even the length of time you must keep them? If you are in business and do not know, here is a refresher. If you are just getting started then you are forewarned of the types of documents and the timelines you must keep them on hand. I have included a Recordkeeping List in Section 5 in the Appendix.

15. Internal Revenue Service (IRS) and Your Business

It is important to know and understand that all applicable laws and governing rules are in place to make sure that everyone, business owner or employee, is operating within these guidelines. Everyone has a part to play in the success of any business endeavor. In order for this success to manifest, all parties must function within the scope of the law. If these guidelines and laws are ignored, there can and will be consequences. Please reference the Publication list in the Appendices Section of this book.

These consequences can include job loss, business shutdown, financial ruin, personal medical issues such as depression, to name a few. One other important piece to bear in mind is the possibility of jail time. Take a look at one such sector – healthcare. Many business owners, doctors included, have committed fraudulent acts against their clients and the government. These individuals are now serving many years in prison. You do not believe this? Just Google 'healthcare fraud' and see what you find.

CHAPTER 3

Business Financing
Myths and Misconceptions

The recent financial meltdown on Wall Street was a sobering reality and a wakeup call for many businesses and individuals. Even before this event, many small business owners were having a hard time accessing the capital they needed. Banks were lending to businesses that posed the least amount of risk. This has always been the bank's mantra—least exposure to RISK.

In many instances, these businesses did not obtain the amount they were originally seeking. Understanding how banks operate when dealing with businesses seeking capital is critical for many business owners. There are many factors to consider when you have a need to approach a banking institution for traditional financing.

The traditional lending institutions have guidelines to follow in determining whether you are a viable candidate for their money or not. They will assess all aspects of your business and you personally to screen against their list of requirements, in order to help them make a final decision.

Being a small or startup business makes it even more difficult for the banks to lend you anything. There are not many banks willing to even look at your loan request if your business has not been up and running for at least three years with good balance sheets and great cash flow. You must realize, banks "look back" at past history, while alternative sources want to know what you plan to do in the future. Banks need stability. Remember RISK. In order for banks to finance your business, they will only accept stable companies in order to feel secure that their loans will be repaid. Not to say that a startup business would not pay its bill, but from a risk perspective, the banks will absolutely not lend to a business in this position.

Many business owners consider financing to be the biggest factor in their business. Financing plays a major role in any business! Not having enough cash flow in place can put a lot of strain on you, the business owner. How you deal with your financial needs is important in your ability to access the capital you need.

Myths and Misconceptions

Individuals who listen to the myths and misconceptions listed below will be in for an unpleasant surprise when seeking financing. Here are a few M & Ms, as I like to call them:

M&M 1: The Banks Will Finance Any Business.

Sorry! Not true! Banks are in business to make money like any other business. They have strict guidelines that many new and small business owners are not aware of. These guidelines affect you one way or another. Even if you have been in business past the banks' required two-year minimum to pre-qualify you, you can still have a hard time obtaining any financing help from them.

M&M 2: I Can Start With Venture Capital.

Many of you might be wondering why no one has come forward to fund your idea or current business. You believe very strongly that your product or service is going to revolutionize a particular industry. You believe your concept can take a piece of a multi-billion dollar industry. You have crunched your numbers and know that any investor will make millions or billions of dollars from your idea.

Think about it! How realistic is it that your idea is the next multi-million or billion-dollar project? This is one of the biggest myths out there. You simply cannot and will not qualify for venture capital financing at the onset, and even after you have been in business for many years, you still might not qualify for this type of financing. Venture Capitalists (VCs) have tightened their requirements during the downturn, as well. Prior to the economic upheaval, many entrepreneurs could not qualify for VC Financing. Even more importantly, you need to realize that venture capital sources require that you give up substantial equity (ownership) and possible financial control in your business. Many business owners are simply not prepared to do that.

If you still strongly believe VC financing is the way to go, you might want to spend some time watching the show, "SHARK TANK", on ABC-TV on Fridays at 8pm. (Be sure to follow the Twitter Handle @ SharkTankABC and the Hashtag #SharkTank during the show. It is a great way to connect and learn more.)

Why should you watch this show? If you have never tried this financing option but feel you should, this program will give you a good taste of what it could be like when you stand before a group of Venture Capitalists. They will eat you alive if you are not prepared. You must have historical data to back up your request, and must have generated a realistic amount of money prior to approaching a VC. You must also be able to think on your feet and learn the art of negotiating.

M&M 3: I Don't Need Outside Financing.

For business owners who believe they can operate their business without outside financing and have the money to do so, great! To those of you who have financed your business out of your own pockets and have been on the financial roller-coaster ride, I am sure you have experienced times when you felt like throwing in the towel because of the financial pressures. Guess what? This is the time to research alternative financing. You should not use your own money once the business is able to obtain its own financing. Using "Other People's Money" (OPM), including the banks, can help to maximize your profits and launch you even further than you ever dreamed.

M&M 4: No One Will Finance A Startup Business.

Wrong! That is absolutely not true! Startup businesses can obtain financing. You just have to be resourceful and know what is available. The financing that small, startup business owners can qualify for depends on a number of variables. Those variables include the type of business, how you plan to operate the business, the people or companies you plan to do business with, and so on. Being a small business or startup does not necessarily disqualify you. You need to have a great product and know the right sources to get what you need.

M&M 5: I Can Get Grant Money To Start My Business.

The question is often asked, "Can I get grant money to start my business?" The straight answer to this question is "NO". There is no grant money available for businesses that operate as 'for-profit businesses'. Whether the grant is being offered by the government or a private organization, your company cannot qualify if you are not a 'non-profit' or 'not-for profit' entity.

Grants are created to solve a specific social or economic need. They are granted to organizations that can put the funds to good use in solving the needs or issues affecting a community or economically disadvantaged group. If your idea or current business does not fit the status of 'non-profit' or 'not-for-profit', then do not waste your time seeking this kind of financing.

In order to be classified as a 'non-profit' or 'not-for-profit' organization, you must have filed for a 501(c) or 501(c)(3) tax-exempt status. To learn more about these types of organizations, please visit the IRS's website at the link below to learn more about creating such an entity. Be sure to seek legal advice also. http://www.irs.gov/charities/index.html

M&M 6: I Can Get An SBA Loan

Many business borrowers believe this myth to be true. Not everyone can qualify for a standard loan. The same is true for the Small Business Administration Guaranteed loans. In order to qualify for an SBA guaranteed loan, a business owner must apply to an approved SBA loan provider; in most instances, these providers are banking sources or other certified lenders.

Once your loan request has been reviewed by the approved SBA banking source, they will then decide if you fit the SBA Loan Guarantee option. This simply means that the source you approached liked your loan request but they are not willing to finance you solely through their bank or company. This is where the term "RISK AVERSE" comes in. Traditional lenders are not willing to risk their capital, so when they get a request they like but do not feel comfortable financing it, they will use options such as the SBA Loan Guarantee. The SBA will then be on the hook for a portion of the loan it guaranteed if you do not repay the loan.

M&M 7: I Can Borrow To Pay Myself

Borrowing money for various business needs is understandable. Trying to borrow money to pay "you" is not. Lenders are not interested in how much you want to pay yourself. They are interested in your commitment to the business and the viability of the company with or without their loan infusion. Whether you are just starting out or have been in business for years, borrowing money to cover your salary is not the thing to do.

This might not seem logical to you at this time but seriously consider this: would you lend to someone who would prefer to pay themselves first or to someone who wants to make their business as successful as possible? Thinking from the lender's perspective should help you realize that the way financing sources look at any request should be from the standpoint of what is reasonable--and borrowing to pay you first is not one of them.

This is one of the top reasons your financing request would be denied. Lenders usually toss these types of requests in the trash without thinking twice. Do not embarrass yourself by requesting financing to pay yourself.

M&M 8: I Don't Need a Business Plan

You might be under the assumption that if you are not seeking financing, then you don't need a business plan. Unfortunately, that is not true. If you believe you can operate your startup business or current business without a business plan, think again. No amount of experience will be enough to keep you fully on track. Whether you seek out other forms of financing or not is irrelevant. Would you take a road trip without your GPS or road map? The same goes for your business.

In order to truly achieve all the goals you could, writing out your business plan will help you to think seriously about what it is you are doing. It will help you stay on track through strategic planning, goal setting and staying focused on the plan for success. So, if you have been in business many years or just starting out, this is applicable to you. Check out the Business Plan information in Chapter 5 for more.

M&M 9: I Don't Need a Web Site For My Business

The thought that you do not need a web site in today's technologically and internet savvy market must be reconsidered. If you have operated without one, you could lose potential business, credibility and more. One of the first things potential clients will do is check out your online presence. Not wanting to incur the cost of setting one up could hurt you in the long run. Also, when you decide you need to access capital for your business, not having a web site might be a problem for the financing source.

Bankers might not care too much one way or the other, but unfortunately it is a problem for alternative financing sources. These sources want to see your web site up and functioning. This is a part of their due diligence process. They want to see all applicable information necessary on your site. Your online presence is just as important as your local one. Having a website could be the difference between just getting by or making a giant leap in your cash flow.

CHAPTER 4

Your Credit: How Important Is It?

Why is your credit rating so important? Why will no bank lend you money without knowing your credit score and reviewing your credit report? What if you do not want anyone to see it? What if it is not great, or even worse, it is very bad? What if you have some negative items on the report that you have been trying to figure out how to remove?

"I just can't seem to get a loan without it." Is this you? If it is, there are many reasons to understand why your credit score is where it is and what you can or cannot do about it. You must understand that your credit score is vital to borrowing money from federally regulated entities and other financing sources. Banks must mitigate their risk. If you are a high-risk borrower, you will not get a bank loan. I am sure you are aware of this fact, or you would not be reading this book. The credit score levels the playing field by giving banks a standardized measure of an individual's credit worthiness.

UNDERSTANDING YOUR FICO SCORE

Most borrowers cannot qualify for bank financing because of a negative credit history. Your credit report is your lifetime report once you leave high school. It follows you everywhere. If you cannot take care of it, then you will not be able to borrow what you want or need and will not have the ability to demand favorable interest rates when you borrow money.

Many business owners do not know that there are alternative

ways of obtaining financing that do not include your credit score. Depending on your business and how you operate, your industry and a number of other factors, you can obtain financing from non-traditional financing sources even with less than stellar credit.

Are these sources not looking at your personal credit? Yes, they are, but understand that they are also looking at the business, who you are doing business with and not just you. Does it benefit you and the alternative source to help you stay in business? I am sure it benefits both.

Biz Tip:

"Know Your Credit". Do NOT hide from your CREDIT. It is your report for life. You can make it a good one or a bad one.

Be sure to check your credit report annually. Get a free credit report by visiting http://www.AnnualCreditReport.com.

VISUALIZE THESE SCENARIOS

I would ask you to close your eyes for this one but since you have to read on to learn more, keep them open. Visualize these two scenarios. You will fall into one of the two scenes. After reading this, you should have no doubt about your borrowing power.

SCENARIO 1:

Person A has a 10-year credit history. He/she had been good with paying down his/her debt and keeping up with his/her credit status for the first 4 years; then tragedy struck. His/her child got very sick and this affected Person A's financial position to where he/she had to declare bankruptcy. The medical bills had been too much. This lasted for a period of about 3 years. After this period, he/she continued to work on rebuilding his/her life, credit and his/her child's wellbeing.

His/her credit report started showing signs of improvement and he/she had not been late on any bills for the next 4 years.

SCENARIO 2:

Person B has the same 10 year credit history except for a few major factors. The credit report shows a pattern over those many years of payment delinquency and judgments. Many of these judgments involved companies like his/her cell phone carrier, his/her electricity provider or some other vital entity in the daily operations of the ordinary citizen. When asked about this report, Person B did not really have a good answer for such issues.

After reading the 2 scenarios above, think on this, which one is more likely to repay a loan? Which one would be more of a "RISK" when borrowing OPM (other people's money)? Let's go a step further and honestly answer this question.

Are you Person A or Person B?

Now close your eyes. Think on this... If you were the lender, would you lend to you? Based on your answer to the above question, you should have a much clearer picture on how lenders assess "RISK". So, before you apply for your next loan, please be honest with yourself. Take a look at your financial and credit positions before seeking out other forms of financial assistance.

FEDERAL CREDIT GUIDELINE CHANGES

With the changes to the Federal Credit Guidelines, every credit card company must disclose the following:

- Must disclose when they plan to increase your interest rate, change annual fees, cash advance fees or late fees, or any other applicable changes to the terms of your card.

- Must tell you how long it will take to pay off your balance if you make only the minimum payment amounts. Each time you receive your monthly statements, it must disclose this information.

- Your credit card company cannot increase your interest rate for the first 12 months after you open an account; exceptions to this rule include variable interest rate; introductory rates must be at least 6 months; if you are more than 2 months past due or if you are in a workout agreement and do not make payments.

- If your credit card company raises your interest rate after the first year, this increased rate can only apply to future charges. It is not applicable to your old balance.

- Credit card companies cannot charge you more than 25% of your initial credit limit in applicable fees. This does not apply to fees such as late payment fees.

- There are restrictions on over-the-limit transactions, such as opting in to the over-the-limit transactions where the credit card company cannot charge you for transactions they have approved when you did not opt in.

- Protection for underage consumers includes needing a co-signer if you are under 21 and cannot show you can make payments.

- Your credit card company must send your bill at least 21 days before your bill is due.

- Your bill's due date should be the same each month.

- If your bill's due date falls on the weekend or a holiday, you have until the next business day to pay the bill.

- Payment cut-off time cannot be earlier than 5pm on the due day.

- Credit card companies can only charge interest on balances in the current billing cycle.

Visit the Federal Reserve's website to learn more at:

http://www.federalreserve.gov/consumerinfo/wyntk_credit-cardrules.htm

Understanding your FICO score and how the credit reporting agencies operate is vital. Learn about the laws that govern your credit and the credit reporting agencies. You can get consumer information from the Federal Trade Commission to help you more.

FEDERAL LAWS GOVERNING CREDIT AND REPORTING:

Federal laws have been created to help protect the consumer. Consumers have rights to fair and equal credit opportunities without being discriminated against. If you feel a business entity or organization might have violated your rights, please read the applicable law as briefly described below. You may then request a copy of the applicable law or use the internet to access that information.

- ECOA – The Equal Credit Opportunity Act

  The ECOA prohibits credit discrimination on the basis of race, religion, sex, age, national origin, marital status, or if you receive public assistance. Visit www.ftc.gov/credit for more information.

- FCBA – The Fair Credit Billing Act

  The FCBA has established procedures for resolving mistakes on credit card billing such as mathematical errors, failure to post payments, failure to send bills to your current address, charges that you did not make, etc.

- FCRA – The Fair Credit Reporting Act

  Enacted in 1970, the FCRA was created to regulate the collection and use of consumer credit information. It is one of the acts that deals with consumer credit rights and is enforced by the US Federal Trade Commission.

- FDCPA – The Fair Debt Collection Practices Act

  The FDCPA was established in 1978 as Title VIII of the Consumer Credit Protection Act. It was established to promote fair collection processes, eliminate abusive practices in the consumer debt collection arena and provide consumers with a way to dispute and obtain valid information relating to their debt, to ensure accuracy. The act defines the rights of consumers involved with debt collectors and guidelines that debt collectors must follow in conducting business. It also outlines penalties and corrective measures for violations of the act.

- FACTA – The Fair and Accurate Credit Transactions Act of 2003

  The FACTA was established as an amendment to the Fair Credit Reporting Act, which allows consumers to request and obtain a free credit report once every twelve months from each of the three major credit reporting agencies, Equifax, Experian, and TransUnion. There are other major areas in this act, including improvements in use and consumer access to credit information, enhancing the accuracy of consumer report information, financial literacy and education improvement, identity theft prevention and credit history restoration.

"With the idea of improving and expanding our company, a kitchen/bathroom home improvement company based in Northern Virginia, we felt that access to capital was critical to our success. We thought a traditional bank loan would be the answer. This was not the case. In the end, if we had better communication with our loan officer or whoever was helping with the loan, we would have had a better understanding, and possibly, a better outcome.

This is why learning about non-traditional forms of financing is important. We are taking this path as it has more flexibility with more solutions and resources. We have learned so much more about the possibilities and various approaches to moving our business forward. We even have the opportunity of helping our clients while not limiting our capabilities."

Sofia Dolan, Part-Owner,
Richstone Marble and Granite LLC
http://www.richstonegranite.com

- TILA – The Truth in Lending Act

  The TILA, enacted in 1968, is a law that protects consumers in lending transactions. This law requires the lender to disclose key terms and terms. Some of the terms that must be disclosed on the approved loan documents are the annual interest rate being charged, the length of the loan in months and/or years, any applicable fees and whom those fees are paid to.

THE CREDIT BUREAUS

Most businesses report to one or more of the credit reporting agencies listed below. To contact the major credit reporting agencies, see the information below. You may visit their web sites to learn more. The five major credit report agencies are:

EQUIFAX
Credit Information Services
P.O. Box 740256
Atlanta, GA 30374-0256
Phone: 1-800-685-1111
Web Site: www.equifax.com

TRANSUNION
National Disclosure Center
P.O. Box 1000
Chester, PA 19022
Phone: 1-800-916-8800
Web Site: www.transunion.com

EXPERIAN
P.O. Box 2104
Allen, TX 75013-2104
Phone: 1-888-397-3742
Web Site: www.experian.com

INNOVIS

250 E. Town St.

Columbus, Ohio 43215

Consumer: 1-800-540-2505

Business: 1-866-391-5484

Web site: www.innovis.com

MICROBILT CORPORATION

1640 Airport Rd.

Suite 115

Kennesaw, GA 30144

Web site: www.microbilt.com

CHAPTER 5

The Dreaded Business Plan: Why You Need One

Many small business owners start their businesses without their road map—the dreaded business plan. Are you one of them? If you are, take some time to sit down and start writing. Do you believe you can make it without one? The answer is yes, but truly, you could be more successful if you had a plan. You do need one, if you truly want to be successful. You might think you cannot write one, but who knows your business better than you do? Whether you just started or have been running your business for a while, it is vital to have a plan.

You might think that at this point in your business life you do not need to write that business plan. Well, I have news for you. Have you analyzed your business since its inception? How successful do you feel you are? Do you have any numbers to measure your success? Do you feel you could have done better if you had that road map? Most assuredly yes, you could have.

Purpose Of The Business Plan

Your business plan serves a variety of purposes. The two primary ones are for you to have a personal guide and for you to seek outside financing. Writing the business plan for your benefit is extremely important. It gives you milestones to aim for and will assist you in your day-to-day activities in achieving those goals. Following the plan gives you a measuring stick to measure your efforts, drawbacks and/or accomplishments. It helps you determine where you need to put more time, money or other resources to make your business more successful.

You can create this personalized business plan for one year, three or even up to five years. It is up to you. It is usually best to do the plan for at least three years, a better time frame to assess your milestones. There is no hard or fast rule here. You will be updating it regularly, so do not get hung up on the length of the plan in years.

Biz Tip:

Having a Business Plan is Your Road Map or GPS to Success. Would you take a cross-country trip without either one? Be prepared.

Let's look at using the business plan to seek financing. When you walk into the bank, one of the key documents the bank official will ask you for is the business plan, including your executive summary. It is vital for you to have a plan that tells the banker who you are, what your plans are and why you are seeking the bank's money. The banker likes business owners who understand their business and its financial position and are able to show why they would make good candidates for bank financing.

BUSINESS PLAN BASICS

When writing your business plan, there are many things to consider, such as type of business, current and future clientele, and whom the plan is for. If you are one who cannot find the time it would take to write the plan, then write a draft and get an affordable business plan writer to do the rest. Especially if you are seeking financing, this is the time you would want to be putting that little extra cash out to secure a professional writer.

If you are considering writing the plan yourself, great! You can do it! Just get on the Internet or call around, and you will be amazed at the amount of information you can find. You can also find business plan software in stores with templates for you to follow. Here are a few key elements to your business plan.

KEY ELEMENTS OF A BUSINESS PLAN

The key elements of a business plan will vary depending on the type of business you decide on or are currently operating and the reason for the plan. The structure of your plan will primarily be based on the following:

- **Business Description and History** – This section explains in detail what your company does, the goods or services you provide and the historical aspect behind what you do. This should give the reader or lender a good understanding of what your company is about.

- **Business Objectives** – The objectives should be clearly defined. They should be specific, measurable, realistic, and time sensitive. These objectives will help you or the lender know why you want to operate this business or want to improve your current operation.

- **Product/Service Description** – This description should give a clear picture as to the product or service you provide or plan to provide. It should help the reader understand your product or service.

- **Competition** – Researching your competition will help you identify other parties in the same market area. This category will explain how much of a threat they pose to your business or new idea. It is a good idea to get specific data on your competitor, such as services offered, pricing, etc.

- **Marketing Plan** – Your marketing plan is extremely vital to the success of your business. It should include the S.W.O.T.

Analysis (Strengths, Weaknesses, Opportunities and Threats). Your plan will include your client market, competition and statistics, including economic, local, regional and national labor markets.

- **Operating Plan** – Your operating plan will describe how you intend to operate the business or how you currently operate. This will give details such as office hours, location of business, internal policies, customer policies and any other applicable information based on your business needs.

> **Biz Tip:**
>
> *Do not include web links that do not exist or do not work in your market research. You do not know when a reviewer might check one of those links.*

- **Management** – The management section must lay out the organizational structure of the company. It will identify the key roles and individuals assigned to those roles based on your business needs. Your management team should share your vision for the business and be able to fulfill the roles assigned to them.

- **Goals and Strategies** – This section will identify specific goals and strategic ways of implementing and attaining the goals you have set. It is good to clearly define what those goals are, both for your purpose, management and any outside parties to whom you might present your business plan, especially for financing.

- **Financials** – The financial section of your business plan is very critical to the success of your business. The financials help you figure out how much money you need to start, operate, or in some cases, borrow. It is extremely important that you know the numbers in this section. Your financial documents will include the following:

- ○ Startup Expenses (if applicable)

- ○ Cash Flow Projections

- ○ Sales Forecast

- ○ Profit and Loss Statement

- ○ Balance Sheet

- ○ Breakeven Analysis

BREAK-EVEN POINT

In order for any business to thrive or survive, the business owner must know and understand their "Break-even Point". If you are a brand new start-up, please make sure you know this concept inside out. The break-even point for any business will factor greatly into whether or not the business is "Cash Flowing" or just an "expensive hobby".

So what is the "Break-even Point"? This is where your income and expenses meet. When the earnings of your company cover the exact amount of your business expenses, you just figured out your break-even point. If the business did not make as much money as you had to pay out in expenses, then you did not meet your break-even point. If you made more in sales than you paid out in expenses, then you surpassed your break-even point.

This can be unsettling for startups and businesses fighting to survive. When this aspect of your business cash flow can be leveraged, then the point can shift from time to time. This is where you go back to the business operations and determine where or what you can trim down on to meet your break-even point.

For those just starting up, you must do a "Break-even analysis" to establish how much money you must make on a daily, weekly or monthly basis to stay afloat. So if you need $5,000 monthly to cover all expenses, then you must sell products or services generating at least $5,000 monthly, $1,250 weekly or roughly $179 on a daily basis to come out even.

Knowing how you compute this figure and being able to tell a lender what the break-even point is will be very helpful to you and them. They will be able to determine if you know what you are talking about from the review of your financials and how this plays into your business plan. For those of you thinking of seeking out Equity/ Venture Capital, this is a must.

You can and will lose out on gaining much needed capital infusion if you cannot quickly speak to this aspect of your business plan. Take my advice and watch the ABC TV series "SHARK TANK". You will learn a lot. (See reference in Chapter 3, M&M #2)

CRITICAL INFORMATION: 12 MONTH CASH FLOW PROJECTION

The cash flow projection you create is the heart of your business plan. Without the completion of the cash flow projection, you will not be able to effectively complete your business plan. In order to identify the income you would like to see on a month-by-month basis, it is critical that you understand the importance of this document. It shows the flow of money in and out of your business on a monthly basis. If you have more expenses than sales or income, then you will not be in business for long.

You can use this projection against your actual monthly cash flow statement. This will let you know if you are on track with your original projected amounts or if you are high or low on a particular line item.

Your cash flow projection should state the following:

- Cash on Hand

- Income Sales / Revenue

- Expenses such as purchases, wages, payroll taxes, marketing

- Loan repayment (if applicable)

- Owner's withdrawal

- Cash Position

Understanding the financial statements in your business plan is vital. You must know and understand these documents, as they will assist you in getting the financing you need or keeping your business on track. If you cannot explain the financial data you have provided and why they are structured the way they are, the banker will more than likely think you do not know enough about your own business. The banker will not feel comfortable lending to someone who is not completely capable of explaining his or her own financial records.

Using your business plan from the financial perspective in other financial markets is also vital. You can use it to apply for small business loans, commercial loans and venture capital, to name a few. Will you qualify for any of them? Who knows? The only way to know is to find out, so if you

Biz Tip:

Know the meaning and value of your business Cash Flow Projections and Statement. It will define your level of success.

need additional financing and the banks are not of any help, then seek out one of these alternative sources.

Remember, your business plan is just one of the key components that will help you obtain traditional financing. Other key components include but are not limited to:

- Your personal credit score

- Your current collateral

- Your financials

- Purpose of the request

- Loan terms

In understanding how traditional lenders use your business plan, it is important to know the reason for writing one in the first place. It is always good to have one prepared, professionally done if you have no time to write one.

The information provided in the business plan must be detailed enough that it will help you advance your business or help others make better decisions in assisting your company. Remember, you can adjust the plan according to the changes affecting your company.

"The backbone of any business is its financial health. A business cannot survive long-term without it. Depending upon the size of the business and the pace of its growth, a financial check-up with an expert should occur either quarterly or annually. Just like your personal health, if you don't catch a problem early enough, it can be much harder to resolve in a favorable manner. It is up to you to be proactive and keep the financial health of your business fine-tuned."

Barbara Greenwald
Former Small Business Banker
www.sheinwaldfinancialstrategies.com

CAN YOUR BUSINESS MAKE IT?

Understanding the business's financial position is very important. This position will show whether the business is on life support or a thriving, healthy operation. In order to address the sustainability of your enterprise, you must be willing to change with the times, technology or any other shift that could affect your business negatively. With this said, be mindful that you are not trying to catch every wave that comes in. Be mindful of the syndrome of wanting to "drink from a fire hose instead of the garden hose". This is especially true when borrowing OPM – Other People's Money".

Capital infusion is always a good thing if you are accessing it for the right reasons and at the right time. Addressing the necessity of borrowing through a magnifying glass process should put you in line with what you really should be doing. For instance, your business could use the additional capital for expansion or the purchase of new equipment or both. Do you really need to buy the most expensive equipment or start a massive expansion campaign? Or can you segment and sequentially phase in what you need to do and have steady growth instead?

So, be mindful of how you approach your business in today's economic environment. Shifts in the various markets, especially the financial market, will trickle down to most businesses, yours included. How firm your financial foundation is will determine if you are still standing at the end of the ride. Remember, when babies learned to move, they wanted to run before they could even crawl or walk. What happened? They would always fall. Let's not put yourself in the same position, as you would stand to fail.

"Being raised in a family and community of entrepreneurs, I had no other desire but to "do my own thing" while in primary school. I now operate a training, professional development and youth services company. With that said, being a small business owner I experience tight cash flow, access to credit issues, limited human resources and much more. I will reluctantly admit that my personal credit, which suffered while trying to start the business, has presented a challenge for me in pursuing more financing. I was approved early on for a small microloan and had a good experience the first time I applied for a loan.

Today, I no longer want to seek traditional financing. I would consider Factoring or contract financing. I intend to operate as close to a completely self-sustaining business from now on. I did not feel good about the liability traditional financing left behind. I would consider bartering or in-house financing with vendor partners. As a trainer and coach, I completely understand that this will not work for every business. I also understand that I may need to change my position as my business grows."

DeShawn Robinson-Chew, Founder & CEO,
She-EO, LLC http://SheEOacademy.com

SECTION 2

"To find your path to success, address your strengths, weaknesses, opportunities and treats, (Your SWOT) then implement the plan for your success."

~Karlene Sinclair-Robinson

THE TRADITIONAL ROUTE

Many years ago, the traditional way of financing a business was always through the banking sector. With the changing tide of the financial market and the demands placed on business owners, the traditional way of financing an entity has shifted.

As I share with you the ebb and flow of this sector, be mindful of what is happening today. The issues surrounding bank closures, scandals and fraudulent activities are all things you must pay attention to. Does this mean all businesses are doing this? Not necessarily.

In all business dealings, perform your checks and balances to know where you stand. This includes checking out your bank just as you would a new client. Just as the banks regularly check your credit, you should do the same. Be sure to read the "Assessing Your Bank" section in Chapter 7 – Bank Financing.

CHAPTER 6

Small Business Administration (SBA): What Every Business Owner Should Know

When you decide to start a business or seeking to expand the current one, it is helpful to know where to go when you need resources, training and advice. Without this type of assistance, you might not be as successful or you might fail in your business venture. It is a daunting thought to step out in the world of entrepreneurship, especially when you feel you are alone. Without resources and the necessary support, many businesses will fail. Even with all the available resources and support, entrepreneurs must step up and seek out the organizations or companies that can facilitate their needs.

This is where the U.S. Small Business Administration comes in. The Small Business Administration (SBA) is the agency of the Federal government that deals with and advocates on behalf of small businesses nationwide. The SBA was created by the Small Business Act of July 30, 1953. The primary functions of the SBA are to provide aid as well as counsel, assist and protect the interest of small business.

The SBA also monitors trends affecting businesses from employee numbers, annual gross income, number of businesses created yearly, how many businesses close their doors each year and much more. They help business owners by providing all types of services in relation to starting a business and seeking financing.

One of the key functions of the SBA is the loan program it guarantees.

The guarantee program allows many business owners to qualify for loans. In many instances, banks are not willing to risk their capital without this guarantee support.

MYTHS ABOUT THE SBA

There are many myths about the Small Business Administration. Depending on your specific need for their services, you could benefit from learning more about the SBA. Understanding the true mission of the SBA is important. The services they provide are all geared toward individuals starting their business for the first time, current small businesses and much more. Here are a few myths about the SBA that must be debunked.

1) **SBA is a lender.**

    The SBA is often times confused by new business owners, students and individuals as a lender. It is widely assumed that the SBA lends money to businesses. However you look at it, the SBA does _not_; I repeat, DOES NOT lend money! I cannot say it any stronger or clearer than that.

    Understanding the concept of "Guaranteeing a Loan" verses creating the loan is very important. The Small Business Administration is not a lender. When a banker is not comfortable taking the risk to lend to you but feels that your business is solid enough, they will present your package to the SBA.

    If the SBA approves and guarantees a portion of the loan, then the banker will be willing to take on the risk for the portion that is not guaranteed.

> **Biz Tip:**
>
> *The SBA is not a lender. They "Guarantee" a portion of the loan repayment to the bank in case the business owner defaults on paying it back.*

Example:	Loan Request Amount	$500,000
	Sba Loan Guarantee(60%)	$300,000
	Borrower's Investment (20%)	$100,000
	Banker's Investment (20%)	$100,000
	Total:	**$500,000**

The bank will then finance their portion (20%) of the loan along with SBA guaranteed amount (60%). You must provide the balance (20%). If you end up defaulting on the loan, then the bank will only be risking their 20% investment. The SBA must then pay the bank the "guaranteed portion" of 60%.

2) SBA Award Grants to Businesses.

Many startup business owners believe that the SBA award grants to all types of businesses. This is simply not true. The SBA does not award grants to "for-profit" businesses. Any time a grant is awarded, it is given to a "non-profit" or "not-for-profit" organization. The term "business" is often used interchangeably with the 3 sectors. This can create confusion as to which type of company can qualify for a grant. Always keep in mind that grants are awarded to "non-profit" or "not-for-profit" organizations that have identified a social, civic or community need and developed a solution to solve that need.

3) Anyone Can Qualify for an SBA loan.

Wouldn't this be great? Every business qualifying for an SBA loan! This is certainly not true. Not everyone can qualify for an SBA guaranteed loan. You must meet certain requirements such as industry, number of employees, income levels, and any applicable request. If the SBA feels that you are not a good fit, then they will advise the lender accordingly.

How They Work

The SBA works with local and regional financial companies, from banks, Small Business Investment Companies (SBIC), and others by guaranteeing a portion of the loan you, the client, actually receive. If you default on the loan, the SBA will repay the lender the agreed percentage. The SBA also works with Small Business Development Centers (SBDCs) and Women's Business Centers (WBCs) throughout the United States.

This collaboration helps startup companies and minority-classified enterprises, including women, veterans and many other small business entities. If you have just started a business, if you plan to start one or if you have been at your current enterprise for some time and are seeking financing for your business, consider locating the nearest SBDC or WBC in your area. They are extremely helpful.

Statistics via the Bureau of Labor and Statistics (www.BLS.gov) shows that the number of new businesses has been on the decline. See below.

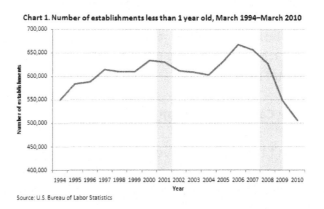

Chart 1. Number of establishments less than 1 year old, March 1994–March 2010

Source: U.S. Bureau of Labor Statistics

The American Jobs Act –
Helping Small Businesses Grow And Hire

"Everyone here knows that small businesses are where most new jobs begin. And you know that while corporate profits have come roaring back, smaller companies haven't. So for everyone who speaks so passionately about making life easier for 'job creators,' this plan is for you."
– President Barack Obama, 9/8/11

Helping small businesses grow and hire is at the core of the American Jobs Act that the President announced. Entrepreneurs and small business owners – America's biggest job creators – are looking to Congress to enact these powerful, bipartisan, specific, paid-for proposals as quickly as possible.

The American Jobs Act will help small businesses continue doing what they do best: create good jobs, drive competitiveness and innovation, and strengthen economic security for the middle class. **The time to act is now. American Jobs Act provisions to help entrepreneurs and small business owners include:**

- **Cutting in half** the payroll taxes (to 3.1%) for small businesses for the first $5 million in wages, targeting the benefit to the 98% of firms that have payroll below this level;

- **Temporarily eliminating employer payroll taxes** for small businesses that create jobs or give raises for existing workers above the prior year (applies to up to $50 million);

- **Extending an immediate 100% expensing write-off** into 2012 to encourage even more businesses to invest in more machinery and equipment;

- **Large tax credits** (up to $4,000) for businesses that hire workers who've been unemployed for 6 months, with bigger credits for hiring unemployed veterans (Returning Heroes Tax Credit up to $5,600) and service-disabled veterans (Wounded Warriors Tax Credit up to $9,600);

- **Billions of dollars in investments** in roads, rail, and airports and the creation of a National Infrastructure Bank;

- **$25 billion for modernizing 35,000 schools**, boosting small construction firms while also strengthening STEM (STEM - Science, Technology, Engineering and Math) education in order to grow tomorrow's entrepreneurs and innovators;

- **Helping small business contractors compete** for infrastructure contracts and get SBA surety bonds up to $5 million;

- **Deploying the power of wireless high-speed internet** to 98% of Americans – including many students, entrepreneurs and small businesses in rural areas – through private-sector auctions of spectrum;

- **Turning job seekers into job creators by making it easier** for States to allow unemployed workers to create their own jobs by starting their own businesses;

- **Increasing skills-based training for youth and adults** to help them transition to the innovation economy;

- **Raising the cap on "mini" public offerings** of small firms from $5 million to $50 million and reducing the disproportionately high costs that smaller companies face when "going public."

In addition, the Administration is moving forward with ideas that don't need Congressional action, including:

- **Paying small contractors more quickly** for the innovative products and services they provide to the federal government;

- **Allowing small business to raise money through crowd-funding** and allowing for new, innovative ways to attract small-dollar investors in small businesses.

Source: U.S. Small Business Administration Web site at: http://www.sba.gov/about-sba-services/199/23001

U.S. Small Business Administration Strategic Plan

Fiscal Years 2011 – 2016

Every few years or so, the SBA releases a strategy document for the current and upcoming years. The three strategic goals outlined for the fiscal years 2011 – 2016 period are not significantly different from those of recent SBA planning cycles. SBA's core objectives of effectively supporting our nation's current and future small business owners and providing assistance to victims of disaster remain unchanged. However, the means for achieving our goals reflect the lessons learned through experiences in serving our customers across the nation and from listening to, and working with, our employees at all organizational levels. SBA's three strategic goals for FY 2011-2016 are:

1. Growing businesses and creating jobs.
2. Building an SBA that meets the needs of today's and tomorrow's small businesses.
3. Serving as the voice for small business.

To read the entire document for this FY 2011-2016 period, please go to:

SOURCE: http://www.sba.gov/sites/default/files/serv_strategic_plan_2010-2016.pdf

---

Small Business Classification

The Small Business Administration also sets the guidelines for small business classification. Each new business must show that it meets a particular classification. The classification requirements vary, based on a number of factors. Those factors include the number of employees your organization has and annual gross income before expenses are paid, to name a few.

Qualifications

Businesses that could potentially qualify for an SBA-backed loan must fit the criteria for each individual loan program. These criteria vary per program, but here is a list that can help you become eligible:

- Must be classified as a small business (Usually under $10 million in annual revenue)

- Must operate as a for-profit and not as a non-profit

- Size of your company

- Percentage owned

- In some instances, the primary owner of the business must be a US citizen

- Most types of businesses, including

  - Service
  - Retail
  - Wholesale
  - Manufacturing

Collateral Checklist

The SBA has specific guidelines as to what type of collateral they will accept based on your loan request. Qualifying collateral must be easily accessible in order for the collateral to be considered acceptable. If the collateral you would like to pledge is tied up in a 401k or mutual funds, neither of these could be considered as collateral based on the nature of them. Items such as your motor vehicle will not be considered.

See the collateral checklist in the Appendices section.

The SBA Loan Programs

The SBA offers a variety of loan programs to qualified applicants. Each program has its own structure and requirements. Here is a list of some of the programs the SBA offers and the maximum guaranteed amount:

- SBA Express (maximum $350K)

- Microloan Program (maximum $35K)

- Community Express Pilot Loan Program (maximum $250K)

- SBIC Program (varies)

- 7(A) (varies)

- 504 Loan Program (varies based on type of company)

- The Surety Bond Program

- Small Office Loan Initiative (maximum $25K)

- HubZone Program

- Small Business Innovation Research Program

- CAPLines (five associated programs)

  - The Contract Loan Program

- The Seasonal Line of Credit Program

- The Builders Line Program

- The Small Asset-Based Line

- The Standard Asset-Based Line

- Export Express (maximum $250K)

- Export Working Capital Program (EWCP) (maximum $2M)

- SBA Ex-Im Bank Co-Guarantee (maximum $2M)

- International Trade Loan Program (maximum $1.75M)

The SBA is there to help a business owner get to the next level. At certain intervals, the SBA is a good fit for your business. Be sure to visit the Web sites listed in the appendix to locate some of the Web sites where you can learn more about the SBA. Based on the information you will learn at the various SBA Web sites, you should be able to figure out if it is the best fit for you. In most cases, these loans do require hard assets as collateral.

Many business owners cannot qualify for an SBA Guarantee loan for a number of reasons. If your credit report and score are not great, this is an option you would not qualify for. The SBA requires that you have more than decent credit. Decent credit to you is not the same to the SBA and the bank you are using. If you do not have the necessary collateral, including the 20 percent deposit or more that is required for a loan to be approved, this will disqualify you. Remember, you must have the necessary collateral, business experience and plan for this all to work in your favor.

All lenders, including the SBA approved lenders, require that you have some "Skin in the Game". This means that you have something to lose in this process if your business fails. It also means that the lenders are not the only ones risking exposure in case you default on the loan.

Do your research prior to applying for a bank loan that the SBA could possibly provide a guarantee for. You will not qualify for an SBA Guaranteed Loan for a number of reasons. Here are a few to keep in mind:

- Credit Score less than 690

- Credit reports with "dings" such as bankruptcies, judgments, liens

- Your industry type could possibly disqualify you

- Business owners' lack of experience

- Negative Cash Flow over a period

- Financial Projections not applicable to the current business model

Of course, once you have done all your research, you can then make the necessary connections to further determine the viability of using an SBA-guaranteed loan. It might be the right fit, or it might not be. Be sure to visit the SBA Web site to learn more. http://www.SBA.gov

**NOTE: THESE REQUIREMENTS
ARE SUBJECT TO CHANGE.**

CHAPTER 7

Bank Financing

You have gone from one bank to the next for a loan to grow or keep your business afloat. You were turned down but are still hopeful that you could keep your business running during tough economic times. What you were not counting on is how much the banking system has changed. Evaluating your financial position prior to seeking bank financing is a must.

Through the traditional route, you could possibly get what you need but more than likely, you will be like the masses, not being able to qualify. Too often though, you have no idea why you were denied the loan. If you can qualify, you will be pledging collateral and investing as much money as possible to make the loan work.

COLLATERAL OR NO COLLATERAL

It is ALL about collateralization. If you cannot provide the applicable collateral to cover the loan amount, in many instances, you will not get approved. Bankers want to see as much collateral as possible. This could include any of the following primary collateral types:

- **Real Estate** – having an unencumbered property based on its value, if applicable to the transaction, would be considered a great asset. If you have a mortgage on the property and not enough equity room that can cover the loan, do not bother using this collateral.

- **Accounts Receivable** – having A/Rs is a plus, especially if the client owing you on those outstanding invoices is the government. Be mindful of the length of time those invoices are past due. Over 90 days can be a problem. Your A/R clients must be creditworthy.

- **Machinery/Heavy Equipment** – having valuable machinery or equipment, just like your real estate, should be "free and clear" of any leveraged debt. If this collateral can be used, go for it. If not, do not consider it.

There are other types of collateral a bank will accept, including certain types of inventory, stocks and certificates of deposit. On the flip side, there are collaterals that are unacceptable.

UNACCEPTABLE COLLATERALS:

- Mutual Funds
- Individual Retirement Accounts (IRA)
- Perishable Inventory
- Jewelry
- Office Furniture

Please reference the Collateral List Type in the Appendices.

UNDERSTANDING THE 8 C's OF LENDING

When banks review a company that is seeking financing, there are eight key areas they use in making a final decision to lend. These are referred to as the 8 C's of Lending. Understanding how banks use the 8 C's of Lending will help you determine whether or not you are a good candidate for bank financing. Of the 8 C's, bankers will focus on Credit, Cash Flow and Collateral as the top three that traditional sources focus on. If these three core areas are deficient, you must reconsider your decision to apply for a loan.

1) **CREDIT** – Your credit score and credit report shows your

personal borrowing history. Your score and credit report must be good to obtain financing through banks, the SBA, and other institutional lenders. If you have not already done so, get a copy of your credit report today and have it analyzed. If you feel there are errors and/or omissions on it, address them immediately to improve your score.

2) **CHARACTER** — Your character is very important, because it will help the banks understand the type of person you are, from being a good citizen to being a good-paying customer. If you are a part of the PTA or sit on the board of any local organization, let the lender know. They want to know what your civic achievements are and any other community involvement that contributes to building up your character.

3) **CASH FLOW** — When banks decide to lend money to any business or individual, the business or individual must show that the available cash flow will be able to sustain taking on the new loan. This means your income minus your expenses must leave room for you to breathe, a fact that gives the bankers a good feel for how well you are doing from a cash-flow perspective.

4) **CAPITAL** — Lenders want to see that you have money to put alongside theirs, because it helps mitigate their risk level. If you do not have the required amount to invest in your own business, it can pose a major problem when securing bank financing. You must understand that no banking institution can or will take on all the risk associated with a particular transaction; furthermore, if you cannot put your own money into the project or business, why should the banks put theirs in?

5) **CAPACITY** — Banks must determine whether a borrower's current position will allow for the new loan. Lenders want to know that the company will not go out of business if they

take on the new loan. The reason for the loan and the potential income from it will also be good factors in judging your capacity.

6) **COLLATERAL** – The collateral provided by the borrower must coincide with what the lenders are looking for when qualifying the candidate for a particular loan. Collateral could include the borrower's home, other real estate, machinery, inventory, and accounts receivable, if applicable. Based on the type of financing you are seeking, lenders can require as much or as little collateral as they deem their risk level requires.

7) **CONDITIONS** – Understanding the current conditions from the lenders' perspectives, borrower's position and the current economic state and how these factors will affect the business is key to making the decision to lend. So, if you were approved for financing eight months ago, but did not take the loan offer, you could potentially not qualify under the current financial climate. Banks have tightened up even more now on their lending requirements.

8) **COMMITMENT** – How strong is your commitment to making your business a success? Your commitment is vital to lenders, in that it shows that lenders have a better chance of being repaid. Are you going to close up shop the minute you hit a rough patch or are you going to stick around? Will you operate the business as a "Hobby" or as a business owner determined to succeed?

Developing a business with tangible assets such as real property or machinery helps demonstrate your commitment, as well. The lenders need to make sure that when they approve your loan you are not going to take the funds and go travel the world. These are things lenders look for and if you are not committed to your enterprise, they will know.

Once you understand all these myths, misconceptions, and the 8 C's, you can use the current conditions to benefit your company. These conditions could include such areas as industry growth, your unique capabilities within your chosen field, population migration, or any other number of changes that present a need, along with you finding a solution to solve a need.

GUARANTEE OPTIONS

The thought of borrowing "OPM – Other People's Money" should put you in mind of what guarantees must you offer. Borrowers who do not read the "Fine Print" will find themselves exposed to additional risks they did not take into consideration. Making sure you understand what documents you are signing will be helpful in the future. There are two (2) types of Guarantees:

1) **Recourse-** Recourse refers to a personal guarantee. This means that you must pay back any loan where there is "recourse". Once you borrow and have breached the terms of the loan contract, the lender has the ability to take you to court, sue for all applicable amounts and will get a judgment against you. The lender can take you to court because you signed the loan agreement that included them having recourse, which is the ability to extract payment.

   If the court finds in favor of the lender, then a judgment will be placed on your credit and against your company, if applicable. This will not be favorable for you in the future if you seek to borrow again. Other lenders will see this judgment as your inability to pay and not finance you. So, if the loan documents do not use the phrase "Recourse", look out for the term "Personal Guarantee". Same thing.

2) **Non-Recourse** - Non-recourse is the total opposite of recourse. This means you and/or your company will not be held responsible for repayment if there is a default, with

one exception: FRAUD. If the financing was obtained under false pretenses, you will be charged or judged accordingly.

If your request was not done through fraudulent means, then you have nothing to worry about. The financing options used in a "non-recourse" method will determine payback options and will clearly state whether there are "personal guarantees" or not. So, be mindful of the types of financing you consider and which guarantee option they would fall under.

Are You Bankable?

After reading the first part of this chapter, you must now honestly ask yourself this question: Are You Bankable? Knowing the requirements for obtaining a traditional loan and the necessity of your business plan, do you feel you are still a good applicant for your bank? If so, great. Go for it.

If you are not sure how bankable you are, here are three things to think about:

1. Start-Up Stage – Pre-Bankable

In the start-up stage, you have more major hurdles to overcome. These hurdles will include not having any business credit history, possible poor personal credit history, no applicable collateral. In order for banks to approve your loan, you must show past historical data that will mitigate the lender's risk exposure.

2. Survival Stage - Turnaround

The survival stage is applicable to all businesses, young or old, especially those severely affected by the ongoing economic downturn. Before the current economic issues, you might not have had a need for any type of outside financing but the ongoing global situation is changing that. With clients taking longer to pay or fewer customers buying your products or services, this is putting a strain on your cash flow and business operations overall.

Surviving through this period will have you making "out-of-the-box" type decisions. If you want to see your business operating for years to come, you will take the necessary steps to continue operating at an optimum but efficient level. If you do not change with the tide, then you could be one of those closing their doors soon.

On another note, it is often said that banks are not lending but that is not true. Banks are lending; you just cannot qualify for the loan. Due to the decisions you might have had to make to keep your business functioning, these decisions in the long term could adversely affect you.

3. Growth Stage – Fast Growing

The growth stage of a business is usually thought of as a good thing. With your business on the fast track to success, growing too rapidly can have its drawbacks. The influx of sales or customers means more production or service hours, more staff and certainly more money needed to operate and keep the business operating optimally. This stage will have you seeking a capital infusion. If you try to manage this period on your own, you could make it or possibly lose everything because you did not reach out for assistance.

So, to determine if you are bankable, answer the following questions:

i.   Did your business operate at a profit for the last three years or at a loss?

ii. Do you have the necessary collateral including at least a twenty (20) percent cash contribution for the loan you seek?

iii. Do you have additional collateral that can be used to cover the balance of the loan?

iv. Does your business plan adequately identify exit strategies for paying back the loan?

v. Do you have good personal credit?

vi. Are you willing to personally guarantee the loan and its repayment?

vii. Are you willing to adjust your expectations if necessary?

The above questions are just some of the ones you must consider prior to seeking bank financing.

"Have a plan for the coming months and years. While any business looking for a loan today has made it through some tough times, we want to know what their plan is going forward. We want to work with companies who have a plan for significant growth as well as contraction. We want to see self "stress tests" and whether they can manage another storm if there is one. We also want to see that businesses have aligned themselves with good advisors (CPAs, attorneys, etc.) that will keep them on the right path.

Cautious optimism – As a business, you have made it through most of a tough storm. Many of your competitors did not make it. There should be opportunity for growth. Put your balance sheet in order so you can seize those opportunities when they come. Evaluate all your advisor, vendor and customer relationships. Are those parties aligned to assist you or not? Replace the ones that do not align with your long term goals."

Eric Myers
TAB Bank

Types of Bank Loans

Banks offer an array of financial products that could benefit your business. These financing solutions are less expensive than other non-traditional options. Here are the average types of loans you can get from a bank:

- Asset-Based Loans

- SBA Guaranteed Loans

- Term Loans

- Business Lines of Credit

- Commercial Real Estate Mortgages

- Equipment Loans

If you can qualify for a bank loan, be mindful of what the requirements are. Be sure you understand clearly what is in the fine print documents you must sign. If your business should encounter tremendous growth in the coming months, you need to understand prior to signing on the dotted line how this could impact your growth potential. Be sure you have a bank that can grow with you.

Please keep in mind though that banks have guidelines that could possible hinder your future growth. If there is no flexibility and willingness to work with you, this could be a big problem. Be sure to question them and get a clear understanding of how they operate.

Who Will Banks Finance?

We already know the answer to this question. Not everyone. Many banks have what is called their "sweet spot" in terms of what will they finance. This is not new. Everyone should have a "niche" that they like and are great at; so do the banks. These institutional lenders will stick to the areas where they have had the most successes. Some love healthcare, others real estate type transactions, while others focus more on "small businesses". Not that they will not finance in other areas--just remember that banks, like other financing sources, have their preferences.

So do your homework before approaching them. Visit their website and call up the nearest branch with applicable questions. And of course, it goes back to collateralization. Make sure you have enough.

"The main problem I see for the last year or so is that financial institutions such as banks simply will NOT lend ANY money to new/start-up companies, even those with signed government and other contracts in hand. Presuming that personal guarantees are also needed (de rigueur), the would-be borrower's credit score has to be nye on to being perfect!

The banks are afraid to make a decision and just keep their $ in their vaults or use it to buy other banks. I've had this conversation with several bankers and they are very evasive about their answers, but it's clear they simply are not getting $ out into the economy. They're afraid to make any decisions (which I point out to them is a decision) and the consequences are that the economy continues to stall with no real new job creation.

An increase in business taxes and getting the top 100+ corporations to pay ANY income tax would also be a boon. For now, they just park their $ off-shore and have the gall to ask for amnesty if they bring it back into this country. Not "buying America" and outsourcing jobs overseas also does not help. I could go on longer, but this is the gist of the problem as I see it. The Women's Business Center/CBP and SBA also have these concerns, although they have to be more diplomatic in voicing them.

Referencing the many cases of indictments by the Federal courts, business ethics and minding such would go a long ways towards avoiding these entanglements.

The best advice I can give a business owner is this: If you have a good product or service, or both, network to let others know. Consider partnering and subcontracting out, so long as the other partner(s) have good reputations."

John Pellegrin, Esq.,
Law Offices of John D. Pellegrin, P.C
www.lawpell.com

Assessing Your Bank

Remember at the start of this section, I pointed out that you should check out your banks, just as they do with your credit, whether business or personal. How do you achieve this? First, visit the financial records posted on their website. Cannot find what you are looking for? Check the "About Us" or "Investor Relations" page on their website. If you still cannot find it, call them up.

These records must be made available to the public and easily accessible. You can also check with the **FDIC – Federal Deposit Insurance Corporation** via their website: (http://www.fdic.gov). While visiting this site, you can also learn about other banks' closings, find information on regulations, identity theft, fraud and much more. For a direct link to the **FDIC Failed Banks page**, visit:

http://www.fdic.gov/bank/individual/failed/index.html

**NOTE: THESE REQUIREMENTS
ARE SUBJECT TO CHANGE.**

The following excerpt is published
with the author's approval.

Pepperdine University State of
Small Business Report EXCERPT

Too Small To Borrow

By JOHN PAGLIA

October 3, 2011 marked the three-year anniversary of President George W. Bush signing into law the Troubled Asset Relief Program (TARP) that authorized the U.S. Government to purchase assets and equity from financial institutions to strengthen the financial sector. In addition to stabilizing the market and protecting taxpayers, the program also aimed to encourage lending to resume to levels before the financial crisis. While the program has been helpful over the short-term in helping financial institutions, the major criticism of government stimulus efforts is that they have done little to make credit available, especially for small businesses.

Since the passage of TARP additional steps have been taken to help small businesses. President Obama highlighted the importance of small businesses in the United States when he signed the Small Business Jobs Act in September 2010; "Now this is important because small businesses produce most of the new jobs in this country. They are the anchors of our Main Streets. They are part of the promise of America – the idea that if you've got a dream and you're willing to work hard, you can succeed. That's what leads a worker to leave a job to become his/her own boss. That's what propels a basement inventor to sell a new product – or an amateur chef to open a restaurant. It's this promise that has drawn millions to our shores and made our economy the envy of the world."

The President's points are spot on, yet the small business economy continues to sputter. Small businesses are not only the anchor on Main Street, but they are also the anchor of our economy. According to the Small Business Administration, small businesses represent 99.7% of all employer firms and employ more than half of private sector employees in the US. They also serve as the major job creation force in our nation. In fact, over the past 15 years small businesses have generated 64 percent of the net new job growth. In terms of Gross Domestic Product, small businesses create more than half of the nation's nonfarm GDP.

The Pepperdine Private Capital Markets Project State of Small Business Report gives capital providers and policymakers a unique look at how small businesses are faring. A comprehensive solution to our economic crisis must include input from small businesses as well as members of the private capital community.

Key findings from the report include:

1. **Overall business conditions are declining and not expected to improve:** The Fall 2010 report indicated that nearly 42% of privately held businesses owners reported that economic conditions improved over the previous six months. While that number increased in the Spring 2011 report to 51%, the Fall 2011 report has shown a strong drop-off of in the number of businesses - only 19% of respondents who say business conditions improved over the previous six months. Looking ahead, just 29% expect an improvement in business conditions over the next twelve months versus 25% who expect a continued deterioration.

2. **There is an aspiration to hire:** The Fall 2011 survey of more than 10,600 small businesses nationwide indicated that 44% of respondents plan to hire in the next six months. Of those that do plan to hire, sales and marketing skills are in greatest demand (47.8%) followed by skilled labor (41.6%)

and service/customer service (38.8%).

3. **Economic uncertainty biggest impediment to growth**: Nearly 38% of respondents believe that economic uncertainty is the largest inhibitor to growth. 26% of respondents said access to capital and 25% said that government regulations and taxes are the number one issue facing small businesses.

4. **Improving access to capital will help create jobs**: Companies with less than $5 million in revenue were clear in the Pepperdine study that of those policies most likely to lead to job creation in 2012, "increased access to capital" was number one (36.0%) followed by "tax incentives" (22.5%), and "regulatory reform" (17.8%). 47.2% of respondents said access to bank loans declined from six months ago versus 10.3% who say it increased.

5. **Businesses that are looking to hire believe training is needed:** Of the privately held businesses that are looking to hire, 48% indicate that sales and marketing skills are their primary focus while 42% of respondents are looking for skilled labor. 82% of respondents believe that they will need to train those they hire.

The current policy response to the Great Recession and tumultuous global economy is vitally important to the success of small businesses and our nation. Through the Pepperdine Private Capital Markets Project State of Small Business Report we gained important insight that will facilitate improved communication between small business owners, capital providers and policy makers. We hope that this information will underscore the importance of privately held businesses in America's economy and will help guide future economic policy.

**PEPPERDINE PRIVATE
CAPITAL MARKETS PROJECT**

STATE OF SMALL BUSINESS REPORT – FALL 2011

*To request the full report, please visit the link below:

http://bschool.pepperdine.edu/appliedresearch/research/pc-
msurvey/form/defaultsmb.htm

SECTION 3

"In life or business, giving up is not an option. You will achieve your dreams when you have laser focus, reaching within and never giving up."

~Karlene Sinclair-Robinson

ALTERNATIVE FINANCING SOLUTIONS

Each financing option in this guide has its own qualifying requirements. These are based on the financing option and funding source you decide to work with. Understanding the processes involved, the options and how to use them will help you gain access to the funding you need now and in the future.

Understanding and accessing these financing solutions does not guarantee that your business will acquire the necessary financing you need.

CHAPTER 8

Personal Financing

Investing your own money to make your dream of business ownership a reality is great. It could be that you need to keep the current business afloat through rough times. Financing your business through direct capital investment is important. This is called having some "Skin in the Game". Lenders like to see that you are willing to invest in your own business and be willing to take on some of the risk.

Your financing could be through monies you have saved up or it could be through a credit card or two. Understanding how best to use these methods to finance your business is vital to keeping your credit intact, along with keeping your cash flowing.

CASH INFUSION

Infusing your business with cash from savings can be a daunting task. You do not know if the business is going make it financially to pay you back. Even with that, you must enact this type of transaction as a loan to the business. Completing a promissory note for repayment should be considered.

A basic note should include the loan amount, interest rate, length of the loan,

> **Biz Tip:**
>
> *Document all personal financial investments to the business as a loan. Keep track of how much you have invested and be sure to communicate this to your CPA.*

current date and all applicable parties must sign the document in case you borrowed from someone else.

Personally financing your business must not be taken lightly. You need to seriously determine what path you will take in financing your business. You get your business plan written and you are now ready to move to the next level, so you pull money from your savings, whether it is your 401(k) or some other investment account, to invest into your unique venture.

CREDIT CARDS

Business owners using their personal credit cards to finance their business can create a nightmare. In one such case, a sole proprietor ended up with just over $210,000 in credit card debt spanning 20 credit cards. Can you image that scenario? Do not let that happening you. This person could not get any type of financing due to this debt load.

Based on your current financial position, using these cards can be a start. Is it the best thing to do? No. Pay close attention to how you use them and do not spend on unnecessary things, events, etc. that could put you in the ditch. This can affect your interest rate and much more.

One thing to note is that, once you start averaging higher balances, the banking source that provided the card is watching. They will check your credit and based on what they find, they can and will reduce your credit card line from where it was to what they feel is reasonable. If you have multiple cards and are using them as such, the banks once again can and will cut the line amount on the cards. The possibility exists that they could turn the amount owed on the credit card into a loan and close out the credit card altogether.

ADVANTAGES

The advantages of using your own money to start or expand your business are essential. They vary from:

- You do not need to qualify for any loans.

- You do not owe others.

- You do not pay any upfront fees.

- You do not have any waiting periods, except those you decide on.

- Your credit is not utilized.

- You do not need to show any collateral.

- You decide when, where, and how, etc.

- You do not give up any control of your business

DISADVANTAGES

The disadvantages of using your own money or credit card are critical to your success. They range from:

- You might be limited to a tight budget to get your business off the ground.

- You could use up all of your liquid assets instead of leveraging your money to the maximum, getting the funds needed to open the business and operate until cash starts flowing.

- If you use your credit card(s), you could be affecting your personal credit score, based on how much you actually spend and how you pay off the balances.

- You will limit your business credit history by not using traditional or non-traditional financing sources that report to the credit reporting agencies.

- You limit yourself and the new business by not developing a relationship with a financial institution that could assist you in the future.

REQUIREMENTS

Because you are financing your business, you will not have any restrictions except for those you put in place. Of course, if you are using a credit card, you are limited to the maximum allowable amount of your personal credit lines and all applicable requirements of that credit card company.

You will have no upfront fees, no credit score issues or collateral issues. You will not have to sign your life away by signing a recourse guarantee (most credit cards function as unsecured loans), and you can certainly finance the business on your own time frame.

CHAPTER 9

Family and Friends

It is great that you want to start or expand your business, but you need some financial help. You decide to introduce your family and friends to your idea and what you plan to do. For the most part, those who believe in *you*, more so than the idea, will probably invest whatever amount they can afford. You and your relatives and friends decide how to embark on such a request, from who can invest some capital and who cannot invest at all.

If you are already in business but have been struggling, you probably would not want to discuss your financial situation with your family and friends. Why? Well, they have seen you struggling to date. Some might be supportive, while others cannot understand why you keep hitting your head against a brick wall. They will probably be wondering why you have not closed the business and moved on, getting a real job like everyone else.

> ## Biz Tip:
>
> *PUT IT IN WRITING! When borrowing from family or friends, have a written agreement! It is a business transaction, so be sure to document it as such. It is the proof that the transaction occurred and what terms the parties agreed to.*

There are many reasons for going to your family and/or friends to help you get your idea off the ground, but you must think really long and hard about it before moving on it, whether it is a new idea or you currently have a business. Remember that these individuals have their own concept of the business or job world.

Many times you are the one with the dreams of making it big in business and not just working at a job that would take you to retirement. Others might not see it this way, so be very careful how you proceed.

PROMISSORY NOTE

When dealing with family and friends, you have to tread lightly. Creating a Promissory Note, as the name suggests, is you promising to repay them for the investment amount agreed to in the signed document. It is important that this document is signed by all parties involved and that there are straightforward provisions in the note, in case you encounter problems later on repaying it. These provisions will help to minimize these issues.

What should be in the note? You will want to make sure the following information is documented in the note:

1. Current Date

2. All parties names

3. Addresses, if applicable

4. Dollar Amount

5. Specific provisions that all parties can agree to

6. Loan term in length, e.g.: 2 years

7. Signatures

8. Notary Signature (that's your third party, if necessary)

You can include any other applicable information you and your friends or family determine is important to you. Tailor-make the note to fit your need.

ADVANTAGES

Asking your family and friends to invest their money to start or expand your business could make or break your relationship, so be very mindful before taking this step in the financing process. The advantages vary from:

- You do not need to qualify for the loan, as they know you.

- You will not pay any upfront fees.

- You do not have any waiting periods, except those agreed upon based on your family's or friends' current financial position.

- Your credit is not used and is therefore not affected.

- You might not need to provide any collateral.

- You and your relatives or friend(s) decide on the terms of repayment

DISADVANTAGES

The disadvantages of asking family and friends to invest their money in your next idea or current business range from:

- You might lose a family member or friend if your business does not succeed as planned.

- You could be limiting your company and its financial requirement to your family's or friends' present financial position.

- Your family or friend(s) might require you to sign an agreement to secure repayment in case you defaulted.

- You will not be building any business credit.

- You limit yourself by not developing a relationship with a financial institution that could assist you with future expansion.

REQUIREMENTS

With your family or friends providing the capital you need, any requirements should be worked out with you and the individual(s), then you should SEEK LEGAL ADVICE! It is good to have a signed agreement, preferably drafted and reviewed by an attorney, to protect all parties involved.

Once all parties are clear as to how much is being invested, the expected interest rate, and length of time that the funds are needed, then you can move to the next step. Get your business moving forward today!

CHAPTER 10

Personal Credit Lines

You might also consider using a personal credit line to fund your business. It's not a bad idea, except that it is much more difficult to get approved if you do not have great credit. Financial sources for this type of financing are primarily traditional lending institutions. Because of the current financial climate, this option might be difficult to access. You might have experienced this difficulty already.

In many instances, though, your local community banks are the best place to start your search to see if you can qualify. The local banks are easier to work with, as you can walk into a banking location and meet with a representative or even a branch manager. If you were to go to a larger banking institution, you might find that it is harder to get the answers or results you might be looking for.

Qualifying for a Credit Line

You may qualify for a secured personal credit line based on your personal credit worthiness and unencumbered assets. Your credit, income and assets are vital in determining how much you can actually get approved for. You might want to take a closer look at your credit report prior to checking out the banks. If you have had any negative items on your credit report, you can check with a credit restoration company before looking for financing.

The type of harmful items that could have a negative impact on the outcome of financing could be bankruptcy, late payments, non-payments, liens, judgments or any other negative or damaging information, so remember to check your credit report and get familiar with it prior to seeking any type of personal financing.

If you are using a broker to assist you, you will be required to pay a broker's fee. In some instances, the broker would work directly with the financial institution on your behalf. In other circumstances, the broker might simply originate some preliminary documentation and then have you work directly with the financial source.

The fee amount you pay the broker is dependent upon whom you are working with, the amount you actually receive and whether you come to a mutually agreeable amount between both parties.

ADVANTAGES

In many instances, if individuals knew they could qualify for and use a personal line as the initial investment to start their business, many of them would not use credit cards as their first resource. The advantages of using an unsecured personal credit line are:

- You may not have to pay any upfront fees, depending on the source. Ask before submitting your application.

- Depending on the source, you could qualify for up to $100,000. Remember, though, with the market as it is, you might not be able to qualify for that much.

- The credit line does not affect your credit until you use it.

- You pay interest only on what you have used and not the actual approved amount.

- The time frame to close this type of transaction is based on the source but often could take up to 6 weeks to close.

Disadvantages

The disadvantages of obtaining or trying to obtain an unsecured personal credit line vary from:

- You must have the necessary and unencumbered assets to qualify.

- You must have a good credit score and history.

- Credit score will have to be at least a median 700 score.

- Your credit history must not have any delinquencies or too many inquiries, depending on the financing source used.

- You must show stable employment.

- The maximum amount for which you could qualify is usually up to around $100,000. This might not be enough, based on your need.

- You will not be building any business credit with this request.

- You may have to pay an application fee, and there could potentially be a percentage fee of the actual amount you receive, depending on the source you use.

- Your credit score and credit history are vital to helping you qualify and obtain the amount you are looking for.

- Your credit history must not have any negative information, such as charge-offs.

- The length of your employment history is also a mandatory requirement, as each financing source must mitigate its exposure to risk.

- Your current revolving debt is also assessed and used to help determine how much you qualify for.

REQUIREMENTS

To qualify for an unsecured personal line, you need to keep a few things in mind. Here is a list of things to consider:

- ❖ **Funding Volume:** *Up to $100,000 based on source used*

- ❖ **Upfront Fees:** *Varies per source*

- ❖ **Qualifications:** *Your credit status*

- ❖ **Credit Score:** *Minimum 700; again, check your source*

- ❖ **Documents Required:** *Credit report is a must for this type of transaction*

- ❖ **Collateral:** *This loan is tied to your credit and good faith that you will repay the loan.*

- ❖ **Guarantee:** *Required; based on financing source*

- ❖ **Time To Close:** *10 to 20 business days*

**NOTE: THESE REQUIREMENTS
ARE SUBJECT TO CHANGE**

CHAPTER 11

Home Equity Lines of Credit (HELOCs)

Home Equity Lines of Credit, better known as HELOCs, play a vital role in helping entrepreneurs finance their business endeavors. Many businesses got started through this type of capital investment. Prior to the housing meltdown, many homeowners had a HELOC. During the downturn and job losses, some homeowners had to resort to using their lines to pay bills and meet essential needs.

With today's declining home values, getting a HELOC might not be as easy. If you own your home and have the equity value in it, you could qualify for one. You must keep in mind though that banks approve these lines based on the current value of the property minus the current mortgage debt. If there is not enough room to create a line, you will not be approved.

Equity Formula Example:

> Current Home Value $ – Current Mortgage Debt $
> = Equity Portion $

If there is enough "equity" in the home, then you can qualify for the line. There is a set percentage that banks will calculate against your equity to come up with the HELOC amount. Please realize that the percentage could vary depending on the bank.

HELOC Formula Example:

Equity Portion $ x Bank's Approved 70%
= HELOC Amount $

You must also consider the Loan-To-Value (LTV) ratio. A LTV of 70% is the percent banks like to work with. For some, the LTV could be as low as 50%. A line amount can be as low as $10,000 or as high as $500,000, depending on the bank you are working with. There are a few banks that will go up to $3 million.

Property Types

Properties considered as primary or secondary residences are the main types of properties used to secure a HELOC. The bank will consider up to 4 properties, that is, the home owner can be approved if they own 1-4 properties.

- Primary Residence

- Secondary Residence

Unacceptable property types include the following:

- Homes for sale

- Mobile homes

- Properties under construction

Advantages

Using a home equity line of credit can have several advantages. They include:

- They offer flexibility.

- You can use the checks just like a regular checking account.

- You can access your HELOC account online.

- You can always convert the balance on the account into a fixed loan with set payments.

- Some banks offer fixed rates.

DISADVANTAGES

The disadvantages of using a HELOC vary, such as:

- You might not qualify for a HELOC based on your current housing market.

- You must show employment stability as part of qualifying.

- If you close the line early, per the contract you signed, you might have to pay a termination fee.

- Mobile homes are not acceptable property types.

- You will not be establishing business credit by using this form of financing.

REQUIREMENTS

The requirements for HELOC's vary based on the source you are using. Pay close attention to the requirements and additional details provided by these sources.

❖ **Funding Volume:**   *Based on home equity value and the bank's LTV percent*

❖ **Upfront Fees:**   *Based on banking source; many banks are not charging a fee.*

- ❖ **Qualifications:**   *Good credit score/history; must own primary or secondary residence; proof of income*

- ❖ **Credit Score:**   *Must be in good standing*

- ❖ **Documents Required:**   *Proof of property ownership; property insurance; -proof of income*

- ❖ **Collateral:**   *Your house or secondary property*

- ❖ **Guarantee:**   *Yes, you will have to provide personal guarantee*

- ❖ **Time To Close:**   *Based on the bank you use*

**NOTE: THESE REQUIREMENTS
ARE SUBJECT TO CHANGE**

CHAPTER 12

Peer-To-Peer Lending

By now you should have heard of the term 'Peer-to-Peer lending'. If you have not, then you are one of the millions that are still in the dark about this unique financing concept. If you have heard of it, great! Did you check it out? Have you used this type of financing? If you have, was your experience good or bad? Whatever your experience, be sure to share it online so others can learn from someone who did it.

Peer-to peer lending has been around for many years. It is a process whereby a group of people comes together to lend money to each other. The number of individuals joining forces varies depending on how they formed the group.

In the last year and a half or so, many online peer-to-peer groups have been created and have been extremely successful. It is changing the face of consumer micro-financing and bringing it to a whole new level. These websites allow you to borrow or become an investor with as little as you want to put in. You can be a part of a group, e.g. a real estate investor group, lending to individuals who have such a need, or it might be a small business group, primarily looking for persons wanting to start a business or expand their current one.

In some third-world countries, this type of micro financing might be called "partner" or "susu", (a term in Ghana which means "small small").

There are slight variations to this type of financing in different countries in that the actual transactions could be considered mandatory savings. "Partner" is used in other parts of the world but mainly in the Caribbean. It does not take place online but instead is transacted through local individuals who might know each other and trust that they will receive their funds or "draw," as it is referred to.

Biz Tip:

Peer-to-Peer lending is one of the easiest ways for ordinary people to do extraordinary things. Lending to help others through leveraging many individuals reduces "RISK".

This process helps ordinary individuals save for unexpected expenses, pay for their children's education, plan for an event such as a wedding or vacation, or just build a nest egg for their future retirement. With this type of transaction, each individual is required to put into the pool a specific sum, e.g. $20.00 per week, fortnight, or month. This amount is agreed to prior to the start, along with the number of individuals involved.

Let's say there are twenty individuals involved, each contributing $20.00 per week. Each week an individual will receive a "draw" totaling $400.00, so for twenty weeks, one of the partners will receive this sum each week. At the end of the twenty weeks, the cycle can repeat itself, if all involved want to continue or it might increase in numbers of people or in the dollar figure, as more people hear about it. It helps them save on a compulsory basis. This way they can plan for life's challenges.

For the sake of this book, we will focus on the online peer-to-peer lending programs for their advantages, disadvantages, and requirements, so you do not get confused with the variations that occur in other countries.

Who Uses Peer-to-Peer Lending?

This financing method is another form of micro-investing at its best. When ordinary individuals cannot qualify for bank financing, through this form of investing, many can get access to the money they need. So, who is using this concept to get the funding they need? People from all walks of life are making use of this. It is amazing to see that individuals investing as little as US $25 can make a big difference in someone's life or business.

Here is a small listing of who is using Peer-to-Peer Lending:

- Students

- Retirees

- Single Moms

- Couples getting married

- Startups

- Small Businesses (all types)

Is this a comprehensive list? Absolutely not! But it sure gives you an idea of who is making good use of such an opportunity.

Becoming a Lender

How cool would it be to start lending small amounts of money to multiple individuals? Or would you rather lend a lump sum to one person? If you had a small amount of money you could invest in this market, would you? Consider the "Risk" of lending a large amount of money to one person verses tiny amounts to many individuals. Reducing the risk of you not being repaid is important.

This is a really good way of investing in others. You can set up a small amount to invest in this market and an even smaller amount to invest per individual. I say, do your homework and if this is a good fit, go for it. Make sure to check these sites out carefully and when you do decide to start investing, do so with your eyes wide open.

Lending Sites

There are two major sites in the US that offer Peer-to-Peer loans. These two sites have both been assessed by the Securities and Exchange Commission (SEC) and are still up and running after their review. I have profiled one of the sites: Prosper.com. I decided to do so after watching this site when it had funded US $29 million to now over US $400 million. Considering that these loans are no more than $25,000, this is amazing to say the least.

LendingClub.com

This peer-to-peer lending site has funded the most to date and is the second oldest such site. They have funded over US $805 million during the period from 5/2007 to 8/2012. The maximum loan size is $35,000 and your credit score must be above 600.

Check them out; they just might be the answer to your financing needs.

Advantages

The advantages of peer-to-peer lending are great for some, while others might find it not as helpful. They include:

- You can obtain a loan much more easily through the online peer-to-peer lending sites.

- Your credit does not need to be A+ to obtain a loan.

- You do not have to meet as many stringent guidelines as compared to the banks.

CORPORATE PROFILE

PROSPER MARKETPLACE, INC.

In 2006, I discovered this online site that was lending money to all sorts of borrowers. At the time, they had loaned out US $29 million. At the end of July 2012, Prosper.com had loaned out U.S. $375 million. This is considered a lot of money. This is even more significant, in that, you can only borrow up to US $25,000.

All the loans approved have been that amount or less. Another important factor is that these are loans made by ordinary individuals and investors alike lending to their peers. This is a perfect example of people being creative when there is a need that is not being fulfilled.

Prosper.com is one of the largest Peer-to-Peer lending sites online with over 1.4 million members. They are also the U.S. first lending site of its kind. It is only accessible to residents in the United States. They lend to individuals and business owners. Many small businesses have now turned to sites like Prosper in order to access capital since traditional banking institutions have tightened their lending requirements.

To learn more about Prosper, please visit:
http://www.Prosper.com

- You can request a loan for a really small amount.

- The length of time to repay the loan and the interest rate you receive can be well worth your time checking out peer-to-peer lending sites.

DISADVANTAGES

The disadvantages of peer-to-peer lending range from a variety of small ones to really large ones, such as:

- Limited amount you can borrow—usually no more than $25,000.

- Most of these online sites do require your credit information to determine whether they can lend to you or not.

- Your credit record dictates your interest rate and how much you can receive.

REQUIREMENTS

The requirements for peer-to-peer lending vary based on the source you are using. Pay close attention to the requirements and additional details provided by these sources.

❖ *Funding Volume:*	*No more then $25,000*
❖ *Upfront Fees:*	*None to date; check your source*
❖ *Qualifications:*	*Credit score*
❖ *Credit Score:*	*Minimum 600; again, check your source*
❖ *Documents Required:*	*In most instances, your credit report will be needed.*

❖ **Collateral:** *This loan is tied to your credit and good faith that you will repay the loan.*

❖ **Guarantee:** *Required; based on financing source*

❖ **Time To Close:** *7 to 14 days*

NOTE: THESE REQUIREMENTS
ARE SUBJECT TO CHANGE

CHAPTER 13

CROWDFUNDING

If you have not previously heard the term "Crowdfunding", you just did. You might be wondering what this is. Whether you know about or not, it is a financing methodology that is changing the way businesses, non-profit organizations and individuals access the money they need as you read this. Understanding this way of raising capital for all types of ventures is vital in today's financial market.

Crowdfunding has taken the financing and innovation arenas by storm. To make a point, even the U.S. Congress has taken notice of this term and financing concept by addressing the U.S. Securities and Exchange Commission (SEC) guidelines governing raising capital for a return on investment.

The history of crowdfunding did not start with the internet. Just like Peer-to-Peer lending, crowdfunding uses a crowd of people to finance various requests. These requests could include product development projects, business expansion ideas, music, art, film and other hard-to-finance industries.

It is important to note that when individuals cannot access the financing they need to bring their ideas, products and services to market, some creative genius or group will figure out a way. This is history repeating itself. When traditional lenders are not willing to risk providing financing in these areas, people will get creative. This is why people are collectively raising millions of dollars through numerous sites like www.IndieGoGo.com, www.Kickstarter.com, www.RocketHub.com and many more.

These sites are helping to create a shift in how everyone from individuals with medical bills to business owners trying to stay afloat to the musician or film producer or even the student with the next big idea can access capital. This is so big that we are now waiting to see what the United States Congress and Senate plan to do with the Federal Securities Laws and how they apply to Crowdfunding and how this affects those investing in this market.

WHAT IS CROWDFUNDING?

Crowdfunding is the concept of using a crowd to finance your project, idea, business or non-profit organization. This concept has leveled the playing field for many individuals who could not get access to the capital they needed to move their business or idea forward.

This financing option is now widely being used as a way to pre-sell goods and ideas. This is a great way to test if you have a good product or idea before trying to mass-produce it. Like so many that have failed to raise money through conventional means, individuals and businesses who do not give up can now try this method.

In order to be successful at crowdfunding your idea, product or need, you must decide on which platform you will use, such as IndieGoGo or Kickstarter. The site you use should accept projects in your field. It is pointless to research and put together a project request when the site you have selected is not applicable to your market. For instance, if

Biz Tip:

The Crowdfunding concept allows you to raise much needed capital through "Pre-Sales". It is NOT for you to ask individuals or investors to invest cash in your business or idea. You MUST offer something in return.

you are a business owner, you would not want to approach a site like Kickstarter while you could be a good candidate for IndieGoGo. Remember, each source has their specialty. So be mindful of this before wasting your time.

Once you have decided on a site and know what you want to request the funding for, be sure to approach the amount you need in a serious light. If you think you need $500,000 but could start with a project request of $50,000, start with the lower amount. You will have to market to your target audience and not every project gets the amount they seek.

Check the site you are using to make sure that at the end of the timeline, you will receive the amount pledged minus the site's applicable fees. Some sites will only allow you to receive the funds if the project is fully funded. There are sites that give you the opportunity to select whether you want to have a "Flexible" funding option or the full amount.

Make sure you pay close attention to the site's rules and be sure to read their "Frequently Asked Questions". The FAQs answer some of the major questions that most users would have.

MAJOR CROWDFUNDING PLAYERS

- **IndieGoGo.com** – considered the world's foremost leader in the crowdfunding platform, it has helped to shape the way for many other such sites. This site allows almost anyone from around the world to create and launch his or her campaign. It does not have a specific category like other sites. This can be great for many who would normally be turned down by other sites.

- **Kickstarter.com** – is also considered one of the big players in the crowdfunding arena. They have specific criteria you must meet before your campaign can be launched on their site. They have niche areas they specialize in, so if your project does not fit, do not waste your time submitting a request. If you do, go for it; you could raise substantial amounts of money for your project, product or for whatever your reason is for launching a campaign.

- **RocketHub.com** – is also a worldwide crowdfunding platform with a focus on artistic, philanthropic, entrepreneurial and scientific type launches.

- **40Billion.com** – is considered the first crowdfunding platform for U.S. small businesses and startups to raise much needed capital.

USING CROWDFUNDING

Crowdfunding is not for everyone. Your idea or product might need to be tweaked or you might need to develop a better marketing strategy to make it work. If you are looking for a "Get-Rich" scheme by raising funds and not delivering a viable product or service through this method, be mindful that the government is watching and people will report you if you defraud anyone of his or her money.

Using crowdfunding to finance your project can certainly get you to the next level. When you offer incentives for specific pledged amounts, please keep in mind that at no time should you offer any future financial incentives. Rewards must not be in the form of cash. The rewards could be anything from specific items such as the actual product you are developing, additional items you can think of and even offering to provide some type of service. You can even get donated items that can be given to the individual pledging support.

Make sure you have done your research prior to using a specific site. If you are a charity seeking funding, use a site applicable to your type of need. If you are a musician or business owner, please do the same.

Advantages

Using crowdfunding to fund your financing need can be an adventure in itself. If you are willing to learn and use it according to the crowdfunding site, then the possibility exists that you could be one of the lucky ones. Here are a few advantages that might be useful to you:

- More web sites are offering this financing method.

- Many more industries could successfully get funded including hard-to-finance markets like film and music.

- You could potentially receive much more financing than you asked for.

Disadvantages

Crowdfunding is great for those projects or requests that fit the source or crowd being tapped. As with other forms of financing, this one has its drawbacks. Here are a few disadvantages you might face:

- The site you select for your crowdfunding opportunity might not be the best fit.

- The project might not be what the crowd is looking to fund.

- You might have requested too high an amount.

- The site most suited for your request might not allow flexible funding.

Requirements

The requirements to access crowdfunding will vary. This is based on the site you use for your project financing. Each crowdfunding site will specify the type of projects that can be posted. Some will even have to approve your request before it can go live on their site. Here is a basic layout of requirements that could be applicable to the site you use:

- ❖ **Funding Volume:** No minimum or maximum. This is based on your project and amount you need to bring it to market.

- ❖ **Upfront Fees:** *Fees are applicable per the website you use. Pay close attention to whether you have to pay a higher fee if you are not fully funded.*

- ❖ **Qualifications:** *This is based on the crowdfunding site you decide to use.*

- ❖ **Credit Score:** *Not applicable*

- ❖ **Documents Required:** *You will need to provide things like credit report and business plan for this option. The information you share with your participants can include links to information about you or your product, and any other information you can share with the crowdfunding audience.*

- ❖ **Collateral:** *You will need to provide incentives for people to pledge to support your project, e.g.: participant pledges $100, you should provide something near or around the value of said amount.*

❖ **Guarantee:** *In the crowdfunding financing model, you must provide the incentive items you offered at the time of funding, e.g.: if you state that participants will receive a copy of your printed book upon publishing if they pledge $25, then you MUST provide said book once it is ready and available.*

❖ **Time To Close:** *The timeline for this option is according to your needs. You can end a project funding in 30, 60, 80 and even up to 120 days. The maximum on this is determined by the web site you use.*

**NOTE: THESE REQUIREMENTS
ARE SUBJECT TO CHANGE**

CHAPTER 14

Business Credit Lines

This is not a viable financial option to consider for a brand new startup during the current financial climate. Business credit lines are offered by a number of banking institutions nationwide. They offer credit lines to businesses based on a number of factors but specifically to entities that have been in business more than two (2) years.

A business owner seeking this type of financing will certainly have to seek out a traditional financial source initially; as such a source would be able to offer lower rates. These lines are easier to obtain, due to the type of qualifications required.

The banks will assess a company's past growth over a period of two years or more. They will assess the viability of the company from the data collected and determine the maximum amount they will approve. The approved amount is based on a percentage of the company's annual gross income in conjunction with the credit risk assessed. This figure could range from ten to twenty percent of the business's annual gross income.

> **Biz Tip:**
>
> *When banks approve a line of credit or any other loan for your business, please pay close attention to the fine print, especially where "Recourse" or "Personal Guarantees" are concerned.*

Based on the changes in the banking sector during the past few years, secured business credit lines are tied to tangible unencumbered assets. If you do not have the necessary collateral to satisfy the lender, you will not be able to qualify. Conversely, unsecured business credit lines do not require collateral. This is solely based on your business financial position and your ability to pay the line if you use it.

It is important to note that though banks operate under the FDIC and SEC guidelines, they have their own internal operational policies. Based on these policies, what you would receive at Bank of America will not be the same as Wells Fargo, or SunTrust, for that matter. Do not leave out your local area banks when considering an unsecured line or the nearest credit union. They just might be the answer to your financing need.

Sources and Line Amounts

Banks offering credit lines have their set minimum and maximum amounts. Here are a few of the major banks line offerings:

Bank of America	$25,000	Not specified
BB&T	$10,000	$50,000 Unsecured $500,000 Secured
Capital One	$10,000	Not specified
M&T Bank	$25,000	$500,000
PNC	$5,000	$100,000
Wells Fargo	$10,000	$100,000

Last updated 7/29/12

Additional Sources:

With the increased demand for access to capital through unsecured lines, many reached out to the traditional sources and failed. If you are still seeking an unsecured line and feel you could still qualify, here is a possible source for you. Visit www.MyCompanyFunding.com.

CORPORATE PROFILE

ELAYAWAY, INC.

Prior to 2005, the concept floated for some time that there had to be a different way to help individuals wanting to travel who could not afford the vacation cost. This idea was the birth of eLayaway. That is, eLayaway.com. What is that you might ask? It is an online site dedicated to layaway services. Our company, through the website helps its customers finance and pay for goods and services they need.

This service is similar to layaway services at walk-in stores available to consumers. eLayaway.com is helping many online customers across a wide cross-section, while providing its vendors with a clear and concise opportunity to maximize potential customers. This helps the vendors who would normally have not accepted the customers who could not or did not want to pay full price up front or pay with high-interest revolving consumer credit.

We allow our customers and vendors the opportunity to use our website to facilitate the buying and selling of products and or services. The customer gets to purchase necessary goods or services that they might not have been able to afford otherwise through installment payments applicable to their budget, and does so for a nominal fee.

Sergio Pinon, CEO, Vice Chairman & Founder,
eLayAway, Inc. www.eLayaway.com

Rates and Annual Fees

It is important to note that some banks will charge an annual fee for the line. This is separate and apart from the interest rate you pay on the line as you use it in your daily operations. So be sure to ask around as to who charges an annual fee prior to accepting a credit line from a given bank.

The rate you will be charged on a line will be based against the Prime Rate plus a variable rate. This rate will be calculated based on your financial position.

Advantages

There are many advantages associated with obtaining an unsecured business credit line, such as:

- Easy application process

- No collateral needed for unsecured lines

- No business plan required

- Fast access to working capital

- Unlike a loan, you only pay interest on the principal amount you use.

Disadvantages

Unsecured business credit lines do come with some disadvantages. Many financial institutions will review your request, but here are the disadvantages and why you might not qualify:

- Your personal credit is required; this is mandatory.

- Your credit score (FICO) in most instances must be above 700.

- Your credit report must be clean and free of any negative information, such as bankruptcy, judgments, liens, late payments, collections, etc. If you had these negative items on your credit from years ago, consider credit repair prior to applying for this type of funding. (These items often remain on your credit report for up to 10 years.)

- You must be in business two years or more.

- Your business must have a good business credit score, otherwise referred to as your Paydex score. This report must also be free of any negatives such as any Uniform Commercial Code filings against you and your business.

- The qualified amount you will receive will be approximately ten to fifteen percent of your company's annual gross income.

- You must present your profit and loss statement and balance sheet.

- You must provide any additional documentation the financing source deems necessary.

Like many other financing options, unsecured business credit lines have their unique requirements. These requirements are not beyond the prospective applicant's reach. It is all in how you assess what you are willing to do to obtain the working capital you are seeking.

REQUIREMENTS

The financing requirements for unsecured business lines in today's market are extremely steep. Prior to the financial crisis of 2008, there were easier ways to obtain an unsecured line. In today's market, you must be diligent.

❖ **Funding Volume:** *The funding volume is based on a*

percentage of your annual gross receipts. For example, let's say you qualify for this option. Here is a breakdown example of what you could receive:

BUSINESS GROSS = $1 million
QUALIFIED PERCENT = 15%
APPROVED LINE = $150K

❖ **Upfront Fees:** *With this option, in most cases, you are not charged any upfront fees by the financial institution. If you are working with a broker or a business consultant, you still should not have to pay any upfront fees. You will pay a closing fee to obtain your unsecured line though. This fee can be paid either directly from the line at closing or by paying with a check associated with the line.*

❖ **Qualifications:** *Your business qualifies for an unsecured business credit line based on these factors:*

- *Two (2) years or more in business*
- *Personal Credit score—700 minimum*
- *Clean credit report including no bankruptcies (check with your bank)*
- *Business annual gross income helps determine the amount you would receive*
- *Banking transaction statements*

❖ **Credit Score:** *Check with your local banks, as they all have various minimum score requirements.*

❖ **Documents** *Each lender has its own style in its*

Required: requirements and how it assesses its risk exposure. It will request documents like the ones listed here:

- Principal's personal credit score and report. Any individuals with more than ten percent ownership must also present their credit reports.
- Annual gross income for the past two to three years
- Current profit and loss statement
- Current balance sheet
- Clear copy of a current driver's license
- Bank statements and/or credit card transaction statements can also be requested.
- Tax returns are required.

For this option, the financial source will certainly also want to review your assets but might not require them as collateral.

❖ **Collateral:** Unsecured lines do not require collateral; Secured business lines will require collateral.

❖ **Guarantee:** Yes, you will have to sign a repayment guarantee. This guarantee will cover the amount you used on the line.

❖ **Time To Close:** The time to close an unsecured line transaction is based solely on the bank you use.

NOTE: THESE REQUIREMENTS
ARE SUBJECT TO CHANGE

CHAPTER 15

Microloan Programs

Microloans, as the name suggests, are loans up to $35,000 made to qualified business owners, especially small and minority business owners. These loan programs are offered throughout the country from a variety of sources. There are many private companies and nonprofit organizations that offer microloans. They are geared toward promoting entrepreneurship by assisting startup companies with initial startup capital or for business expansion.

They are applicable to any company or individual who qualifies based on each lender's specific criteria. Micro loan lenders have their own requirements, from what your credit score should be to the variation in the application process. These loans provide the much-needed capital that many people cannot qualify for through conventional banks.

Some examples of micro loans are the Patriot Express Loans and Small Office/Home Office (SOHO) Loans. These loans are offered not just to startup companies but also to other qualified borrowers who want to expand their businesses. The SOHO loans are offered to business owners who operate from a home office. Borrowers must show their need for this loan and their ability to repay, and must be willing to present any applicable documentation required.

Keep in mind, though, with the current economic situation, most financing sources are requiring full documentation to prove that you are worthy of their financing. The amount you qualify for is based on the criteria set forth by the individual source you are using; on average, Micro loan lenders will lend to businesses or individuals who would not normally qualify for bank financing.

Top Micro Lender:

ACCIONUSA.org – is considered the top micro lender in the U.S. They have provided over US$119 million in funds to over 19,000 small businesses nationwide. It is worthy to note the impact this organization has had on businesses and the local economy over the years.

Biz Tip:

A Micro Loan is the ANSWER to many small business owners financing needs. You just have to learn how to qualify for it and make it work for you.

Accion USA provides loans from as low as $500 to a maximum of $50,000. The minimum credit score they accept is 525. Yes folks, you read that correctly—525. There are other factors to consider including if you have had a bankruptcy in your past history, late mortgage payments, outstanding medical bills and so on.

Qualifying for an Accion USA micro loan can make the difference to you achieving your financing goals. So, consider all options carefully, do your homework and plan accordingly.

Advantages

There are many advantages to using micro loans. In determining if this funding alternative is most suited for your business, review the following advantages:

- The requirements and documentation needed for this type of financing do not always include tax returns and corporate financial documents.

- You do not have to borrow more than you need.

- This type of financing is easier to close.

- The time frame to close this type of transaction can be from two to four weeks.

Disadvantages

There are several disadvantages when seeking a small microloan for your business, including:

- Your credit and credit history are vital to your obtaining this loan.

- The maximum amount you can qualify for might not fit your needs.

- It takes approximately two to four weeks to close.

- Depending on the financing source you use, you might have to pay upfront fees.

- You might need to present other collateral, not including real estate.

- Once you are approved and have access to the loan, you have additional debt to cover.

- Collateral required could include your vehicle or other tangible assets.

Requirements

Many micro loan lenders, including the SBA-approved lenders, have specific requirements. These requirements vary from:

❖ **Funding Volume:**   *Up to $35,000*

❖ **Upfront Fees:**   *Based on source used*

❖ **Qualifications:**
- *Your credit report and score are critical.*
- *Use of loan proceeds*
- *Type of business you operate*

❖ **Credit Score:** Minimum 640; again, check your source

❖ **Documents Required:**
- *Your credit report is a requirement.*
- *Copy of your state identification, such as your driver's license*
- *Business plan is required, depending on the lenders' specifications*
- *Articles of incorporation or other corporate documents.*
- *Tax returns are required.*

For this option, the financial source will certainly also want to review your assets but might not require them as collateral.

❖ **Collateral:** Based on source used--accounts receivable, business equipment, motor vehicle, etc.

❖ **Guarantee:** Required, based on financing source.

❖ **Time To Close:** 6 Weeks – 10 Weeks or more.

NOTE: THESE REQUIREMENTS
ARE SUBJECT TO CHANGE

CHAPTER 16

EQUIPMENT LEASE FINANCING

Operating a business, whether small, large or in between, is hard work. Whether you are starting a small business, are a self-employed business owner, or own a mid to large sized business, you will face challenges daily, especially on the financial side. If financial issues are not handled properly, you could undermine your business's financial well-being and hinder its growth.

Business owners like you need to make investments in some type of basic equipment and/or supplies to facilitate your business's operating needs, such as increased growth. Often you will put your own money into your equipment purchases. All of this spending can add up quickly, depleting your cash reserves. This is one of the worst mistakes a business owner could make.

Many business owners are not aware of the benefits of using lease options to help grow their business. Most owners have been misled into using unsecured credit lines as their primary financing option, which is not a good idea. When you obtain a credit line, you are building up personal debt that can lower your credit scores, which will make your purchasing power much weaker.

Leasing is a rapidly growing method of acquiring the necessary equipment a business needs. Leasing allows you to use the equipment you need for a set period of time while benefiting from having your cash flow unaffected.

Some reasons why you might consider an equipment lease option are:

- You lack sufficient capital for the full purchase.

- You do not want to use your own funds initially.

- You cannot qualify for bank financing.

- You do not want to restrict your growth potential.

- You want tax incentives.

- You want to use the equipment for a limited period of time.

In today's competitive marketplace, you must stay ahead of the game if you plan to succeed. Large companies lease their equipment all the time. Airlines, tour companies, trucking and construction firms--you name it, lease their equipment.

> Check with Your CPA -
> **IRS Section 179**
> Expense Deduction

Types of Leases

There are essentially four types of leases available to the equipment buyer. Each type of lease is based on what fits your company best.

Operating lease: An operating lease is sometimes used interchangeably with a tax lease. The financing instrument that closely resembles an operating lease is an automobile lease. Essentially, an operating lease does not fully amortize until the lessor realizes the asset's residual value. To qualify as an operating lease, the lease must meet a handful of standards, including for the lessor to be "at risk" for not earning the full investment in the lease, including yield, based on the lease payments plus the forecasted residual value of the equipment.

TRAC Lease: TRAC is an acronym for Terminal Rental Adjustment Clause and is reserved for leases covering titled equipment. Unlike operating leases, TRAC leases allow the lessor to fix the amount of the forecasted residual as an addendum to the lease contract yet still qualify as a tax lease.

Leverage Lease: Most commonly used for leases involving large dollar amounts, leverage leases have more than one party investing in the lease, with a finance investor (or investors), who earns income from a stream of payments, and the equity investor(s) realize the residual value of the equipment much in the same way an annuity would be earned.

Finance Lease: The finance lease is also referred to as a "money-over-money" lease. The lessor earns its target yield primarily from the amortization of the payment stream. With the finance lease, the end user (lessee) is using the instrument with little outlay of cash and paying for the equipment over the term.

How do you get started? First, you need to figure out your business equipment needs and then put together an itemized list with cost factors. Obtaining photos and costing from the vendor, if necessary, is very helpful. Communicate with a leasing company and/or broker related entity that can assist you with this type of transaction. Get your business moving forward today!

TYPES OF LEASEABLE EQUIPMENT

The list below is representative and does not constitute the only types of equipment that can be leased.

Addressing Machine	Material Handling
Collating Equipment	Medical / Dental
Computers	Office
Appliances	Office Furniture
Copy Machines	Printing
Industrial / Heavy Duty	Food/Restaurant
Construction	Store Fixtures
Farm	Telecommunications
Software	Others

If you believe equipment lease financing is an option for you, be sure to do your research, check with your bank and then look at all your options before moving forward.

ACQUISITION METHODS

Alternative ways of obtaining the equipment your business needs are cash outlay, bank loans or leasing. With the cash purchase, you spent capital that could have been used for something else and you ended up restricting your cash flow. The equipment will also lose value before it is fully depreciated. Banks tend to be very restrictive and can be unattractive sources to finance equipment. They have an extensive application process; stringent guidelines, higher payment methods and limited program options, and their initial deposit requirement are high.

Leasing often is the most attractive option. More than eight percent of all businesses in the U.S. use lease options. There are many benefits to using this financing option, including tax incentives (be sure to check with your CPA).

ADVANTAGES

Using equipment leasing offers many advantages for many

businesses. The advantages of using this option vary based on the alternative financial source you use, the cost factor and the type of equipment you are obtaining. Here are a few advantages:

- Payment options that fit your budget

- Potential tax benefits—see IRS Section 179 (check with your CPA)

- Little to no money out of pocket resulting in cash conservation.

- It helps to preserve your credit line.

- It is convenient and provides for a simplified process.

- You can receive up to 100% financing (if applicable).

- You can acquire or upgrade the equipment you want.

- You can divert your cash to expand your business.

- Leasing gives you a competitive edge.

- You don't have to maintain older obsolete equipment

DISADVANTAGES

Equipment financing affords the business owner a few options, but there are a few drawbacks.

- Because leasing means you do not own the equipment, you do not benefit from taxable depreciation or purchase.

- The overall cost of the equipment can be substantial over the period of the lease.

- The actual ownership of the property does not come to you until you have completed the payment process, and only if you have a lease/purchase option.

- You do not build equity in the item you actually lease, so you cannot use it as collateral.

- Early cancellation fees do apply, and they can be expensive, so be sure to check the fine print before you sign a leasing agreement.

- If your leasable equipment has any maintenance issues, you will have to fix it or have the leasing company provide service. This can be expensive.

REQUIREMENTS

The following items are considered when reviewing your credit application or approval:

❖ **Funding Volume:**   *$1,000 minimum; no defined maximum*

❖ **Upfront Fees:**   *None to date, but check your sources*

❖ **Qualifications:**   *Must show need for approved type equipment and show the capacity to repay*

❖ **Credit Score:**   *Minimum score 620*

❖ **Documents Required:**   Startup Businesses

- *Business plan and résumé showing industry experience*
- *The last two years' personal tax returns on all principals*
- *A personal financial statement on all principals*
- *Copy of vendor's invoice or proposal, if available*
- *Personal credit on all owners, officers, partners or members*
- *Time in business under current ownership*

- *Business Checking and Supplier References*
- *Industry, equipment type and age*

Two Year+ Established Businesses

- *Year-to-date interim financial statements, including profit and loss and balance sheet*
- *Your last two years' business tax returns or financial statements*
- *The last two years' personal tax returns on all principals*
- *A personal financial statement on all principals*
- *Copy of the vendor's invoice or proposal, if available*

❖ **Collateral:** *The collateral needed for this financing option would be determined by the source used.*

❖ **Guarantee:** *This is dependent on the source used and how much is being requested.*

❖ **Time To Close:** *10 – 25 business days normally*

**NOTE: THESE REQUIREMENTS
ARE SUBJECT TO CHANGE**

CHAPTER 17

Factoring and Accounts Receivable Financing

Business owners tend to confuse accounts receivable financing with factoring. Yes, they are extremely similar in their approach to funding, but with slight variations. These variations can cause you either to save money or to spend more. It all depends on how you look at the whole picture. It also depends on where you are with your business.

Accounts receivable (A/R) financing tends to concentrate on businesses averaging approximately $500,000 or more monthly. If you are averaging this amount, then you seriously might want to consider this financing option versus a bank loan.

What this means for you is this: if you plan to use A/R financing for an extended period of time, let's say one year or more, then it makes good business and financial sense to use A/R financing. If you plan to use A/R financing for only one or two months, then you should consider factoring.

Accounts receivable financing uses a process whereby you use all your receivables (all of them!). Think of putting all the receivables in a pot and you can only access a portion

Biz Tip:

Factoring your Accounts Receivable is the 'Sale of an Asset'. You receive cash from the sale. This does not create 'Debt' on your Balance Sheet.

of the amount on a daily basis. You will be able to use a portion of your outstanding amount before your client pays, as seen in the example below.

The basic example below shows how an accounts receivable funder would finance you based on your outstanding receivables. Of course they go over many criteria to determine that they are able to facilitate this option for you.

For example:

- Monthly Receivables   = $500,000

- A/R Financing   = $500,000

- A/R Financing Facility   = 80%

- Reserve Amount   = 20%

- **Monthly Draw Amount**   **= $400,000**

- **Reserve Amount**   **= $100,000**

Your own and your clients' creditworthiness are extremely vital in being approved for A/R financing. If your clients' credit worthiness is not good, you will have a problem, as this option pools together all your receivables. All your clients' receivables are lumped together for the funder to finance you.

APPLICABLE LAW

The Assignment of Claims Act of 1940

~~~~

This law allows for the legal sale of invoices.

FACTORING

Factoring is the financial process whereby the sale of an invoice for upfront payment occurs. This sale involves you (the customer), your client (business party who owes you or your company money) and the financial source (funder) that is willing to purchase the receivables. Depending on how you are introduced to the factoring financial product, there might be a fourth person involved, a consultant or a broker.

Factoring has been around from many years. Throughout the history of this industry here in the United States, countless companies have used this financing option to expand their companies or keep them from going out of business. Many of the large firms nationwide continue to use factoring as their business need for cash flow continues. Some of these are companies you use every day or buy products from on a regular basis.

Small to mid-size firms have now started using this option, especially with the current tight credit market. With banks not lending as they used to, more and more of these companies must open their eyes to the realization that they should seriously consider it for their business, because many big businesses use factoring and grow tremendously.

For example:

Invoice	$1,000
80% Advance	$800
Reserve	$200
-2.5% Discount	-$25
17.5% Reserve Rebate	$175

Factoring Myths

- Factoring Is a Loan

  When business owners are first exposed to the concept of factoring, they seem to think of it as a loan. Well, it is not, because it does not increase the liabilities column on your balance sheet. Remember that your accounts receivable are assets that you can sell, and so factoring is the transaction that involves the sale of those receivables.

- Factoring Creates Debt

  Once again, remember that factoring is the buying and selling of invoices or accounts receivable. Going back to the balance sheet, your receivables were originally in your assets column. Now that you have sold them, where do you think the gain from said sale should go? Well, of course, *the monies received from the sale of your receivables still stay in your assets column.* So really, it cannot be considered a debt or loan, for that matter, as it never entered your liability column.

Specialized Factoring

- Construction Factoring

  Construction factoring is the factoring of accounts receivable invoices within the construction industry through niche-based financing sources. This industry is very diverse and complex. It has a wide array of businesses, including electricians, painters, asphalt suppliers, demolition companies and many more vying for financing. This diversity of vendors and how construction companies operate and bill in conjunction with a particular project can create certain drawbacks when seeking this type of funding.

Progress billing refers to billing of a job at various stages of completion. Each construction job may have a need for an electrician, plumber, mason, and painter, to name a few. As each professional gets finished, he or she then bills for services rendered.

Financing for construction receivables is made much easier with factoring. Many companies have the ability to access this option, but only a limited amount of funding sources will take on construction factoring. This is primarily due to the high risk associated with construction projects and the progress billing methodology within this industry. The factoring process helps many smaller and larger construction companies continue to stay in business.

- Medical Accounts Receivable Factoring

Medical factoring, as the title suggests, is the financing of medical receivables. Many medical practices, hospitals, home health agencies, rehabilitation centers and others have used this option to keep their business running optimally. The ability of a hospital or medical practice to factor their receivables is vital. In some instances, it is the only way they can meet their payroll or other overhead expenses.

This factoring option is probably one of the most difficult to approve, because of the issues and processes associated with the insurance industry, Medicare or Medicaid. This is not to say that many companies do not qualify for medical receivable factoring; it is just not as straightforward a transaction as a commercial type would be, because of the intricacies of the insurance industry.

Working with Medicare, Medicaid or any health insurance carrier takes time and patience. These organizations have their own particular way of doing things, and all others must abide by these rules, in order to do business with them. Sometimes it can be time-consuming. Of course, all invoices to these companies must go through strict guidelines to alleviate the fraudulent billing claims they receive from time to time.

Primary Medical Insurance Payers

- Medicare
- Medicaid
- Insurance Companies

- Healthcare Factoring

  As part of the factoring concept, medical factoring is very specialized based on the primary source of payment coming through the government run programs, Medicare and Medicaid. With that said, "Healthcare Factoring" deals with the factoring of invoices in the healthcare sector where the payers are not Medicare or Medicaid.

  Any healthcare company that invoices other non-government clients and needs access to capital through their receivables can sell these receivables to factoring companies in this niche market.

Primary Users of Healthcare Factoring

- Medical Services Providers
- Businesses, e.g.:
  o Staffing Services
  o Transportation Services
- Government Contractors not billing the primary medical insurance providers

FACTORING KEY PHRASES

- **Account Debtor:** Refers to another name for the client's customers; the entity that the factoring funder collects from

- **Accounts Payable:** Money the client pays out or owes

- **Accounts Receivable:** Money received or owed to the client

- **Advance Rate:** The percentage of money that a factor advances its clients upon the sale of its invoices.

- **Discount Fee:** The fee that the factor charges when purchasing an invoice.

- **Reserve:** In Factoring, this refers to the percent advanced, minus the factor's discount fee.

- **UCC-1 (Uniform Commercial Code-1 Financial Form)** This is the legal document a factor files with the applicable Secretary of State office advising them of their interest in a particular individual or company's accounts receivable as detailed in the document pursuant to a prior agreement. This serves as notice and protection for the factor, by placing them in first position against the receivables.

- **Verification:** The method by which a factoring source validates invoices they purchase by communicating with the payer of the invoice to verify that the goods or services were in fact, provided.

ADVANTAGES

Many business owners still do not realize the major advantages available to them when they use a program like accounts receivable financing. Below you will find a list that can help you determine why you should use it.

- Factoring your receivables is fast and easy.

- It frees up your cash flow.

- It allows for greater flexibility.

- Factoring gives you immediate access to cash upon the sale of an invoice.

- You can receive cash TODAY instead of days, weeks, or even months down the road.

- It helps you increase your sales or take on new contracts.

- Factoring helps to build your business credit score by leveraging your customers.

- It does not create liability on your company's balance sheet.

- Factoring gives you the ability to perform credit screening and monitoring of your clients.

- It allows you to plan ahead for future contracting opportunities or other business-related ventures.

- It allows you to keep the equity in your business instead of giving it up.

- Factoring allows you to grow your business.

Disadvantages

This is the one time I can say there are not many disadvantages to using a particular financing option. Many times when a business owner decides not to use factoring, it is not necessarily the financing option that they have a problem with. The few drawbacks I can think of are:

- The minimum and maximum funded amount is mandated by the financial source you use.

- In some instances, if you do not have a consultant to help you select a funding source and you decide to use any source you find, it might not be a good match up.

- The funding source you use might not be able to handle the growth you can achieve while using their financial services.

- Prospective clients might not be well informed on how the factoring process actually works.

- The number one disadvantage would be that some business owners do not know much about the topic and believe everything bad they have heard about it, without getting better educated on the topic.

REQUIREMENTS

Most accounts receivable funding sources require the same paperwork. Depending on the type of accounts receivable you are selling at a discount, the factoring process varies, but not by much. Here are some additional things you must be aware of:

- ❖ **Funding Volume:** *No Minimum, No Maximum*
- ❖ **Upfront Fees:** *Depends on Alternate Funder used*
- ❖ **Qualifications:** *MUST produce invoices to creditworthy buyers*
- ❖ **Credit Score:** *Not a requirement*
- ❖ **Documents Required:**
  - *Accounts Receivable Aging Report*
  - *Accounts Payable Aging Report*
  - *Fictitious Name Filing, Articles of Incorporation, Bylaws or Operating Agreement*
  - *Corporate Documents*
  - *Proof of 941's-Payroll Taxes*
  - *Any other document that funder requires*

❖ **Collateral:** *Unencumbered Accounts Receivable*

❖ **Guarantee:** *A personal guarantee is not normally required.*

❖ **Time To Close:** *2 Weeks or more*

**NOTE: THESE REQUIREMENTS
ARE SUBJECT TO CHANGE**

CHAPTER 18

Purchase Order Financing

Purchase Order Financing is a type of financing that exists specifically to help a business owner handle a large order. PO financing, as it is sometimes called, is used when the business owner cannot facilitate the funding of an order.

For example, a business selling uniforms to a state governmental agency receives an order for 50,000 uniforms instead of the 10,000 that the agency normally orders. This situation can cause the business owner receiving such a large order to panic if they do not have the financing to deliver the goods. This is where PO financing is very effective in helping the business fulfill orders like these and continue its client relationship.

How It Works

In the example above, the PO financier would help the business owner by advancing to the actual manufacturer or supplier of the uniforms a deposit amount against the cost to make the garments, to get the order underway. Once the uniforms have been made and delivered to the governmental agency and the items have been received in good standing and verified by the agency,

Biz Tip:

Increase your business cash flow with this concept by including "Tangible Goods" as part of your revenue stream. You can then use PO financing to make the transaction work.

the PO financier will then in turn, pay the balance of the cost to make the uniforms to the manufacturer or supplier.

The business owner then has the ability to bill the state or federal government agency or client for the delivered goods while the PO financier waits for the client to pay the bill. The client then pays the bill through the financier, who subtracts its fee amount and returns the balance to the business owner.

Companies that can access this financing option tend to be wholesalers, distributors, resellers, importers or exporters. Other companies can qualify, but it is on a case-by-case basis. The cost to use PO Funding varies per source but is considered more expensive when compared to other financing options like factoring.

SAMPLE TRANSACTION

Getting large orders can create a lot of headaches. This is a good kind of headache to have when you know where to go for financing. Without these types of financing solutions, many commercial transactions would not occur. Here is a sample order from a cred-itworthy client:

> **Biz Tip:**
>
> *Pending orders can be the answer to helping you secure the financing you need. Purchase orders for your products are a good way to help finance your business.*

- ○ Initial order:10,000 Polo Shirts @ $50 each = $500,000

- ○ Manufacturing cost:$18 each including shipping = $180,000

- ○ Client is not willing to deposit any monies upfront

- ○ Purchase Order funder has been contacted; they like

you and approve of your client.

- They request that a Factoring source be put in place at the end of the transaction before they'll go forward.

- You secure Factoring source.

- Purchase Order source then finances the initial transaction by paying the manufacturer $180,000 to produce and deliver the goods to your creditworthy client.

- Client receives the polo shirts in "good standing" and signs off their approval.

- You can now bill your client by invoicing whereby you then sell the invoice to the Factoring source.

- In the meantime, the Factoring source pays off the Purchase Order funder $180,000 plus applicable fees; then advances you the applicable amount per their approved advance rate.

- The Factoring source then waits for your client to pay the bill.

- Once your client pays the invoice to the Factoring source, this funder will then deduct all applicable fees and payments made on your behalf, and send you the "reserve" balance left over.

When you consider using Purchase Order Financing and Factoring, always keep in mind the 'number line'. You have a positive and a negative side. The negative side has 'more risk' while the positive side has 'less risk'. Purchase Order Financing is on the negative side or high risk, for the main reason that the lender is providing funding for you prior to any work being done or any tangible product delivered.

The fees to use this financing service will be much higher than most but the key will be for you to price your product correctly, deliver it in a timely fashion and keep your customers happy. It is important that we not just look at how much things cost but also at how they can help enhance what we are doing.

Advantages

Purchase Order Financing provides a unique way for businesses to secure financing and get their businesses moving forward. The benefits of using purchase order financing vary, based on each individual business owner's needs. They include:

- It allows you to fill large unexpected purchase orders.

- It helps you complete these orders, even when you have the cash flow but do not want to tie up your cash.

- Creditworthy customers make it easier to access purchase order financing.

- Purchase order financing is a fast way to get your products or orders moved very quickly when payment is needed.

- When the banks have turned you down, purchase order financing is a great option for meeting large orders.

- Purchase order financing allows you to finance up to 100% of the goods that need to be delivered to your customers.

- It is great for wholesalers, distributors, resellers, importers/exporters, or other types of businesses.

- It allows you to use other financing options, such as factoring, in conjunction with purchase order funding.

Disadvantages

Even with all the benefits of purchase order funding, there are sometimes disadvantages that may not make it the best fit for your financial needs. These vary, but here are a few of them:

- High fee rates—the fees assessed for the use of PO funding can be high, especially if you are a small business owner.

- You must factor your receivables in order to use PO funding.

- Depending on your business needs, if you do not have a finished product being shipped from a manufacturer or supplier, then you cannot use this option.

This product requires finished goods being delivered from your supplier directly to your customer. This means that if you must assemble or handle the product, you will not be able to use this financing option.

REQUIREMENTS

Purchase order financing has its basic requirements, so be sure to check with the source you plan to use, especially if you are not working with a consultant.

- ❖ **Funding Volume:**   *No minimum, no maximum*
- ❖ **Upfront Fees:**   *Yes, in most instances. Check with your source*
- ❖ **Qualifications:**   *MUST produce invoices to creditworthy buyers*
- ❖ **Credit Score:**   *Based on source used*
- ❖ **Documents Required:**
  - *Business executive summary, including history*
  - *Accounts receivable aging report*
  - *Accounts payable aging report*
  - *Fictitious name filing, articles of incorporation, bylaws or operating agreement*

- *Corporate documents including your Articles of Incorporation and Certificate of Incorporation in Good Standing*
- *Personal financial statements, if applicable*
- *Proof of federal tax ID number*
- *Current bank statements*
- *941s, proof of payments*
- *Contract or purchase order*
- *Sample purchase order, if applicable*
- Your invoice to buyer
- Your supplier's invoice

❖ **Collateral:** *Unencumbered accounts receivable*

❖ **Guarantee:** *A personal guarantee is not normally required.*

❖ **Time To Close:** *2 Weeks or more*

NOTE: THESE REQUIREMENTS
ARE SUBJECT TO CHANGE

CHAPTER 19

Merchant Cash Advance
(Credit Card Receivable Financing)

Merchant cash advance or credit card receivable financing re-fers to the financing of future expected credit card transaction payments. This is factoring with a twist for companies that use credit card transactions to receive payments. This type of financing is for those who need financing but do not fit many of the other options available, especially when they cannot go to the bank.

Most businesses accepting credit cards for payment are immediately pre-qualified for this financing option. Each company seeking merchant cash advance financing would be pre-approved but must show the capacity to which it can repay the proposed funded amount. Your company might be in a poor state with some obstacles and you could still potentially be approved to receive funding.

What Is A Funder Seeking?

Each financing source has its own method of evaluating your request. The sources look at your monthly merchant volume; your business bank statements; your location, including rental status, if applicable; and a number of other key areas to determine whether or not you are a qualified prospect. The funder will determine from the information presented to them and using a formula for repayment, how much you could potentially qualify for. This option can be ideal for places like restaurants and hair salons that might not qualify for traditional bank financing.

Based on the amount you are seeking, the funding source then determines the maximum it is willing to approve you for, and if there are no unexpected surprises, then you will receive the quoted amount at the time of your pre-approval.

ADVANTAGES

Merchant advance or credit card financing allows for many advantages. The following advantages will be applicable based on your current situation:

- Merchant cash advance affords potential clients a great opportunity to take their businesses to the next level through business expansion.

- This option is not dependent on your personal credit score or your credit history.

- It does not require extensive corporate documentation, such as audited tax returns and business plans.

- If you accept credit cards for payment, it is easier to qualify for a merchant cash advance.

- It is a fast way to receive funding; you can be funded in about seven to ten business days.

- You can pay suppliers and vendors in a timely manner.

- You can increase inventory/equipment.

- You can increase your sales and client base.

- Funds from this financing can be used for unexpected expenses.

- You can fill more orders.

DISADVANTAGES

Merchant cash advance has its share of disadvantages. These disadvantages include:

- You can use credit payment processing and still not qualify for merchant cash advance financing.

- The cost to repay this type of funding can be high.

- The amount you qualify for might not be enough.

- In most instances, you will have to switch your current credit card processing company. The funding source will want you to use one of its own card-swiping machine providers.

REQUIREMENTS

The requirements for merchant cash advances, like all other options, are a source-by-source choice.

❖	*Funding Volume:*	*Maximum $600,000*
❖	*Upfront Fees:*	*In most instances, there are no upfront fees.*
❖	*Qualifications:*	*You MUST accept credit cards as payment from customers*
❖	*Credit Score:*	*Not a requirement but your credit report will be reviewed to help determine your character.*
❖	*Documents Required:*	▪ *Must have a business store-front location* ▪ *Most recent three to four months of credit card statements* ▪ *Most recent three to four months of bank statements* ▪ *Voided check*

- *Copy of business site lease agreement*
- *Authorization to communicate with landlord*
- *Copy of license to conduct business*
- *An enlarged copy of principal's picture ID*
- *Fictitious name filing, articles of incorporation, bylaws or operating agreement*
- *Corporate documents*

❖ **Collateral:** *Unencumbered accounts receivable*

❖ **Guarantee:** *A personal guarantee is not normally required.*

❖ **Time To Close:** *30 days or more*

NOTE: THESE REQUIREMENTS
ARE SUBJECT TO CHANGE

CHAPTER 20

VENDOR FINANCING

When your business has a need to purchase goods, you might not be able to purchase the necessary products upfront based on your cash flow. If you receive a Purchase Order from one of your clients and you know you might not be able to fill it, this form of financing just might be the answer.

Vendor financing is a financing method that is used when you need to purchase tangible products. This form of financing is primarily provided by companies to their customers based on the customers' payment history. So, your credit is an important part of the approval process. The relationship you built with the vendor over the years might also be beneficial. These vendors might approve your application internally or they might outsource it to a vendor financing company or credit card processing firm.

It is important to note that not all product-based companies offer Vendor Financing. Some companies cannot be bothered with the hassle of dealing with business owners who do not pay their bills while others do not want to go through the process of working with a credit card company or other financing source. Others cannot qualify for a vendor financing program through credit card companies and do not want to take the risk of doing it on their own.

The types of companies offering Vendor Financing fall into a variety of industries. These companies could be in any industry ranging from construction, technology, medical, janitorial, or any other that has a product base.

Companies that offer this type of financing can do so in two ways:

1. Credit Card offering

2. Vendor Note (Paper) creation

These methods of financing are based on the individual companies offering their customers the opportunity to do business on credit or what is sometimes referred to as "Payment Terms". If the company offers a credit card, you will have to apply through their credit card processing company first. Once you are approved for a set amount, you now have the opportunity to purchase their products with the credit card. This is like having a store card.

It is always best though to pay off this form of financing as quickly as possible, as it could cost you much more than you originally estimated. *Be sure you know what your maximum credit limit is, the interest rate and any applicable fees for using this type of financing.* One important thing to note--do not sign up for multiple vendor programs if you do not absolutely need them.

If the company offers you terms to pay for the products by creating a vendor note (paper), this note should define the payment terms including the interest rate, length in months and any applicable consequences for not meeting the requirements of the vendor note. Once you have defined your purpose for using it, locating a vendor offering this type of service might not be easy. If your vendor does not offer this type of financing program you might want to ask them if they would consider it.

There are a number of advantages and disadvantages to using this form of financing. Be sure to assess how this will help to grow your business before signing off on using it.

ADVANTAGES

Vendor financing offers a number of advantages that can greatly benefit both the company providing the financing and the client using this form of financing:

- There are flexible payment plans.

- Opportunity to increase spending limits.

- Allows for maximizing your cash flow.

- This financing can be tailor-made to fit the parties' needs.

- Vendors can increase their client base by offering this financing option.

- The client does not have to make large deposits.

- Clients with credit challenges could still qualify for this form of financing.

DISADVANTAGES

The disadvantages of using Vendor Financing can impede your company's progress if not used wisely. Some disadvantages are:

- The vendor has the right to deny your request.

- Your credit report and your personal credit score could deter your approval if the report reflects that you do not care about your credit.

- Your ability to pay will determine your ability to get approved. If you do not have a viable business or cannot prove you have a steady income, then you could be denied.

- The vendor you need to use might not offer a financing program.

REQUIREMENTS

The requirements to use this type of financing vary based on the vendor you work with:

- ❖ **Funding Volume:**   Amount based on vendor source
- ❖ **Upfront Fees:**   *Based on source's requirements*
- ❖ **Qualifications:**   *Vendor-specific*
- ❖ **Credit Score:**   *Varies – as low as 550*
- ❖ **Documents Required:**   Credit Report
- ❖ **Collateral:**   *Not applicable*
- ❖ **Guarantee:**   *Yes, you will have to guarantee repaying this type of financing*
- ❖ **Time To Close:**   *Vendor specific*

NOTE: THESE REQUIREMENTS
ARE SUBJECT TO CHANGE

CHAPTER 21

Asset-Based Loans

Asset-based loans allow businesses or individuals to obtain cash or short-term working capital based on their assets. These assets vary from real estate to accounts receivable and inventory to your machinery and equipment.

In the banking sector, companies that can qualify for this type of financing usually have in excess of $10 million in annual sales and are highly leveraged companies. If you are doing less in annual sales but have the collateral, an asset-based loan is still an option to consider, because of the secondary financing market.

Asset-based lenders are available for companies that might not fit the banking model. Each of these lenders has its own prerequisites for you to qualify for any particular amount. Of course all will assess your current financial position to determine what risk level they are dealing with. They will then use a formula encompassing your real assets, receivables, inventory and any other assets they think are viable.

Biz Tip:

All collateral used in an Asset-Based loan package will be inaccessible for use in any other form of financing. Be sure you know what this means for your business and personal assets.

INDUSTRIES SERVED

Many industries can benefit from the asset-based lenders available nationwide. Asset-based lenders primarily look for companies that have a combination of accounts receivable and other tangible assets. These companies include:

- Manufacturers

- Wholesalers

- Commercial Service Companies

- Contractors

This list is incomplete, so it does not mean that other areas or types of businesses could not use this option. It all boils down to what the client is seeking and what financing is available, as well as whether the borrower takes the necessary steps to facilitate and fill the requirements of the loan.

ADVANTAGES

The advantages of using your own assets to raise the capital you need are great. If you have sufficient collateral to do this without using all of your assets, then go for it.

- It is a great way to raise much-needed capital.

- It provides short-term working capital.

- It can be a fast way to secure the much-needed liquidity that you need.

- You do not need outside investors or long-term bank loans.

DISADVANTAGES

There are many disadvantages of using asset-based lending in securing the capital you need. You need to be cautious, as shown below:

- Your assets are tied up. You will not be able to sell your assets at a later time if you obtained a loan against them as collateral.

- You must have assets that can qualify. Many business owners do not realize that not all items can qualify for an asset-based loan.

- There are high due-diligence fees.

- You must show strong corporate financial statements.

- You must present your personal financial statement, and it too must be strong.

- There is no flexibility when using an asset-based loan. All applicable assets such as real estate, machinery, accounts receivable, etc., will be used as collateral to give you the financing you need.

- It limits your future borrowing capabilities.

- The minimum amount most private sources want to fund is $1,000,000.

- There are a few private financing sources that will go below the above amount, but usually no less than $500,000.

- Banks providing asset-based loans, in most instances, will not go below $10 million. It is not worth it to them. Check with your local banks.

REQUIREMENTS

Each source determines what it requires to make a decision to fund a client. Some have more stringent requirements than others. In any case, you will be asked for both corporate and personal financial statements.

You must present assets that are free and clear, with no liens against your equipment or machinery. Your real estate must either be free and clear or have such a small mortgaged amount that the asset-based loan can facilitate paying it off. To obtain an asset-based loan, the primary requirements are as follows:

❖ **Funding Volume:**   *$100,000 minimum amount*

❖ **Upfront Fees:**   *Yes, based on source used*

❖ **Qualifications:**   *You must have a combination of assets that can qualify, such as:*

- *Real Estate*
- *Inventory*
- *Machinery or Equipment*
- *Accounts Receivable*

❖ **Credit Score:**   *This type of financing is primarily based on the value of the asset or assets securing the loan.*

❖ **Documents Required:**   *List of assets including purchase price, date of purchase and current liens*

❖ **Collateral:**   *Determined by the source being used and the assets you have that will qualify*

❖ **Guarantee:**   *All parties involved must sign a personal guarantee.*

❖ **Time To Close:**   *45 days – 70 days*

NOTE: THESE REQUIREMENTS
ARE SUBJECT TO CHANGE

CHAPTER 22

Commercial Real Estate Financing

Commercial real estate financing is the financing of a real estate transaction during purchase or refinance. This can be a transaction completed with or without cash out to the borrower. The types of properties vary and include hotels, restaurants, apartment buildings and owner-occupied properties. There are conventional loans, acquisition and development construction loans, bridge loans, and hard-money loans. These loans range from small loans up to $1.5 M, mid-size loans up to $3M or large transactions in the hundreds of millions.

Many commercial funders will finance potential prospects regionally, nationwide and even internationally. Each transaction is different. Each funder is different. Banks are a primary source for commercial loans, but there are many other private commercial lenders. These lenders, or funders, as we call them, will fund from as low as $50,000. You just have to know your source and what their requirements are.

A seller, a buyer, a commercial appraiser and the primary lender are the key parties in a commercial real estate financing transaction. This transaction can also include but is not limited to a commercial real estate attorney, bank, surveyor, realtor, contractor and any other professional deemed necessary to complete the transaction.

In the processing of this type of financing, each lender has its specific criteria. Be sure to know what that source is seeking prior to your loan request. Once you have submitted your request, it can be a fast process or a long one, concerning how quickly you can get approved and funded.

There are commercial lenders for all types of property, including farms, hotels, gas stations, residential developments, assisted–living facilities and hospitals. Each source has an itemized list of the types of real estate transactions it will finance and the maximum and minimum it will fund.

As with other types of funding, commercial real estate financing has a number of other types of financing programs that fall under its umbrella. The additional subcategory types have specific ways they can finance a transaction. These vary from hard money, rehab loans, bridge loans, mezzanine loans and commercial venture capital, to name a few.

Bridge Loans

Flexibility and speed are two very important elements to any financing transaction. If these ingredients are not readily available, it can and will cost many thousands, if not, millions of dollars. When a business owner or real estate investor needs to finance a transaction but is coming up short in making the deal work, considering a bridge loan is vital.

Biz Tip:

*If you want to use Other People's Money (OPM), you **MUST** have some "Skin in the Game". The concept of "No Money out of Pocket" is no more.*

Bridge loans have been used to make many loans more attractive to banks and other investors. These loans are not stand-alone options but complement many other options and have helped to save many transactions. So, do not hesitate to consider using a bridge loan when you have leveraged all your collateral connected with all your resources and this is your only alternative. Make it work for you.

HARD MONEY

In the real estate financing world, hard-money financing is one of the most misunderstood funding solutions out there. It is a financing concept that many investors do not realize as a viable option available to them. Hard money works only with real estate. You must have some hard assets to collateralize the loan. It can make a hard-to-finance real estate project a reality. Once the objectives are addressed from both the lender and the borrower's perspective, it can be smooth sailing using this option. It must be a win-win-win all around for all parties involved.

Hard-money financing is fast and gets the job done. What many individuals do not like is the fact that there are high interest rates, and due diligence fees tend to be on the high side. What the individual borrower must ascertain is what hard money can do for them and their project instead of focusing on the fees and the rates. With this said, the borrower must come to the transaction with some "Skin in the Game". This means you must have some 'risk exposure' as well as the lender. Many transactions have failed because the borrower had nothing in the deal.

Seeking to use this option without having some financial or other tangible investment will make this request null and void. You cannot expect the lender to put in thousands of dollars or even millions for that matter, without you having something to lose in case the deal does not work out, or if after closing, the project falls through. Those who are looking to wholesale properties and thinking about using this option must seriously consider how they structure such a transaction. You must make it favorable to the lender in such a way that you will get what you need in the end.

Get with a good source who knows what he or she is doing, and you could potentially have a good partner for your future projects.

ADVANTAGES

It is great if you can qualify for and obtain commercial financing for your project. It goes back to the term "OPM—Other People's Money." Once you have learned how to use commercial financing, it can be a great way to get your project off the ground or see it through to its end. As you can tell, there are many advantages to using commercial real estate financing. Here are a few:

- Commercial real estate financing provides access to liquidity that you might not otherwise have had access to before.

- You use OPM to get your project completed on time and within your projected gross profit margin.

- When you want to do another transaction, you will know where to go.

- The time line for processing your documentation can be very fast.

- Depending on the source you use, your transaction can be completed in a time frame ranging from three weeks to three months, more or less. This time line impacts the interests of both parties involved.

- You have the opportunity to build a relationship with the lending source. This will make future transactions much, much easier to complete.

DISADVANTAGES

As with all the other financing options, commercial real estate financing has its own drawbacks. These disadvantages are more noticeable depending on the source you use. Here are a few disadvantages:

- It is not always as clear-cut as others would have you think.

- The amount you are qualified for could be less than what you need.

- Sometimes the time it takes to go from the pre-approval stage to the funded stage can be months.

REQUIREMENTS

The requirements to fulfill this type of financing vary per lending source.

❖ **Funding Volume:**   *Minimum $50,000; no maximum*

❖ **Upfront Fees:**   *Yes; amounts vary based on the source you use*

❖ **Qualifications:**   *You qualify for commercial real estate financing based on the project you are requesting the funding for.*

Types of property qualification

- *Residential (more than five units)*
- *Commercially zoned properties to include:*
  - Golf Courses
  - Hotel Developments
  - Hospitals
  - Assisted Living Facilities
  - Office Buildings
  - Storage Facilities
  - And Many More

❖ **Credit Score:**   *Your credit score is dependent on the source, but use a baseline of 600 minimum, except in the case of Hard Money.*

❖ **Documents**   *Three years' income tax and*

Required:		*financial statements*

- *Year-to-date profit and loss and balance statement*
- *Personal finance statements*
- *Projected cash flow statements for next twelve months*
- *Pro forma for next twelve months/ length of loan*
- *Federal and state tax information*
- *Collateral sheet*
- *Well-written business plan*
- *Any other applicable documents*

❖ **Collateral:** Real property

❖ **Guarantee:** Yes, depending on source used

❖ **Time To Close:** up to 60, 90, or more days

**NOTE: THESE REQUIREMENTS
ARE SUBJECT TO CHANGE**

CHAPTER 23

Venture Capital

Venture capital or VC funding, is the financing of a particular business by a private investment firm that has the capital and management expertise to back its investment. The VC firm then becomes a partner in your business. Based on this investment and partnership, the receiving company will not have to repay the invested amount. The venture capital firm will be repaid from the capital gains of the company.

When you started your business, you might have decided your company should use a private equity investment firm. If you did seek this type of financing and secured it, you got lucky. I also know you got a rude awakening. Many times individuals get going with the business of creating their new company and have the mindset that they will certainly get venture capital. It's not that simple.

One of the best things you can do to fully understand using this type of financing is to watch the ABC TV program, "SHARK TANK". After seeing one episode of this show, you will know if this financing is what you really need or was just something you were dreaming about.

How to Qualify

Many private investment companies will invest only in geographical locations they like, in industries they love, and in companies where they can see strong returns on their money. These investors vary in their requirements and types of companies or products they will back. Some will invest in technology, healthcare, energy, real estate and inventions of all types, to name a few.

How do you qualify for such a unique investment opportunity? It is based on your product or idea, your experience, your company strength, your financial position and the team you have on board. VC funders very often place more emphasis on the team than the idea or the product line (no matter how breakthrough they are); because they need to know your company can execute on the plan and achieve profitability.

There could be more. Because of the high volume of companies interested in seeking venture capital financing, the private investment sources are even more selective in which companies they accept and fund. Based on industry figures, out of every 1,000 business plans that are submitted annually in the hope of being selected, *only two to four* are selected.

Venture capitalists can help a company expand or get off the ground, and they can help a company make a lot of money. They do so by investing their money, time, staff, market and industry connections and any additional resources to help make their investment pay off. In some cases, they

Biz Tip:

Be real when you seek "Other People's Money", OPM, to finance your business. How much are you willing to give up?

will be directly involved with your company. With some companies, the venture capital firm will be more hands off, while with others, they will provide daily or weekly input in the operations of the company. Most often, they will also have a seat on your board of directors, as well.

One of the hardest parts of obtaining this type of financing is the in-person presentation or pitch you will have to give to sell your idea or product to these firms. Remember first impressions? If your pitch is no good, there is no way you will get a venture capitalist to take you seriously.

STAGES OF VENTURE CAPITAL

- Early Stage
  - Seeding
  - Startup
  - First Stage
- Late Stage
  - Second Stage
  - Third-Stage Financing
  - Mezzanine Financing

INDUSTRY FOCUS

- Technology
- Retail
- Sports
- Internet
- Real Estate
- Medical/Healthcare
- Alternative Energy
- Financial Services
- Cybersecurity

Biz Tip:

Equity or Venture Capital financing is for those companies that can present a viable product. It must have tremendous potential and can show evidence to fit this option.

The above listings are just a few of the areas a venture capital firm might focus their investment and time. Each individual firm has their criteria, so be sure to do your research.

Are You Ready?

Presenting your idea or business to a venture capitalist means that you must be prepared. There are many variables to consider but some of the major areas you must focus on are:

- Commitment – VCs want to see how committed you are to the business at hand. They must know that you want this business or product line to succeed more than they do.

- Management Team – do you have the team in place to make this work? Does the team come with the necessary experience to make this work?

- Product Viability – is the product a viable item that can sell and make money for the investors and shareholders?

- Know your numbers – being able to present and discuss in a brief presentation your financial capabilities with your product or service will give you some edge over others.

- Scalability – is the business or product concept one that will grow? Is there a market for it? How big is that market? Will it continue to grow and how does the business idea fit into this market? All questions that must be answered

- Exit Strategy – what contingencies are in place or have been considered in order to exit this line of investment? You must have a few, not just one.

Advantages

As with any financing source, there are many advantages of using this type of financing. In spite of the ratio going against your firm being selected, if you are selected, here are a number of advantages to take note of:

- Once you are approved for venture capital financing, you will have access to a team of people who are dedicated to the success of your business or idea.

- You will have access to the much-needed capital you need to take your business or idea to the next level.

- The network of connections the VC has can benefit you.

- VC can speedily help make your business more profitable.

- VC firms offer mentoring that helps your business be more successful.

DISADVANTAGES

The disadvantages of VC financing affect each business in a different way. Some of the things listed below might or might not relate to you.

- Not all businesses or industries can qualify for VC financing.

- The rigorous due diligence process VC funders put you through can be extensive, and you still can come out at the end with nothing.

- The length of time due diligence takes can be a drawback.

- The fees VC funders require prior to their due diligence time line can be a drawback for companies that might not be able to afford it or do not wish to pay the fee.

- Most VC's take at least 51% ownership of your company in exchange for funding it.

- If you fail to meet certain post-funding milestones, VC firms will take additional shares of ownership in your company.

Requirements

The requirements for obtaining venture capital are as diverse as the words themselves. Understand your market and do your research before seeking a venture capitalist. Since the recent economic downturn, VC firms have raised their requirements. Very few will now fund startups.

❖ **Funding Volume:** Minimum $100,000 – No maximum

❖ **Upfront Fees:** *YES, amount is based on source*

❖ **Qualifications:** *Management status, business viability, market share*

❖ **Credit Score:** *A good credit score/report is useful*

❖ **Documents: Required**
- *Business plan*
- *Management resumes*
- *Business tax returns*
- *Corporate documents to include current balance sheet*
- *Personal financial statements*
- *List of assets, both personal and business*

❖ **Collateral:** *This is determined based on type of business and venture capitalist you decide to work with.*

❖ **Guarantee:** *In some instances, yes; in others, no*

❖ **Time To Close:** *Anywhere from three months to as long as it takes*

NOTE: THESE REQUIREMENTS
ARE SUBJECT TO CHANGE

CHAPTER 24

IRA Financing

Retirement planning is an important part of everyone's future financial planning process. Looking forward to retiring with some level of comfort is important. Many individuals have 401K or Roth IRA type retirement accounts that they have spent years building up. When you plan out your retirement it is with hope and optimism that you continue to pay into these types of accounts. Otherwise, you might be left with no retirement money when you hit the big number "65". With the stock market fluctuations, you need unique ways to invest your money.

With some retirement accounts, you cannot touch them; that is, use any of the funds, until you reach the age of retirement set by the Government. We've all heard the familiar phrase "substantial penalty for early withdrawal." Do you understand the value and true potential of these types of accounts? Have you any idea or know any of the laws governing these types of accounts?

Often we have no idea of the full potential and benefits of these retirement accounts. Some of you might have considered borrowing against your retirement account while others have actually done so. In order to give you the best information on this particular topic, I reached out to one of the top sources who specialize in retirement accounts and investments.

Further information on this topic will expressly be the views of the writer, Curtis DeYoung, CEO of American Pension

Services.

Do More With What You Already Have

There are trillions of dollars in retirement plans and billions con-tributed to 401(k)s each week. Have you considered using IRAs or 401(k)s to fund your business? If not, you have arguably missed the single most accessible alternative funding source available today. IRAs and 401(k)s are untapped capital resources you must under-stand: knowing what IRAs and 401(k)s can really do enables you to do more with what you already have.

There are several ways you might take advantage of the trillions in IRAs and 401(k)s to fund your big idea:

1. **Genuine Self-Direction**
   a. Be A Lender Or Find A Lender
   b. Closely Held Stock
   c. Partnerships/LLCs
2. **Know The Rules**
   a. 401(k) Participant Loan
   b. IRA 60-Day Rollover
   c. 72t Early Retirement Distribution

Genuine Self-Direction

Self-Directed IRAs and 401(k)s are a gateway to business funding capital because while banks are busy adopting stringent lending practices, self-directed retirement account owners are making hard money loans. While the country waits for their government to cure the economic ills of the world, self-directed IRAs and 401(k)s rep-resent an oasis of opportunity for not only the account owner but also the entrepreneur who understands how self-directed plans can grow their business. Though you cannot use your own self-directed plan to directly benefit you personally, the knowledge that self-directed IRAs and 401(k)s have the flexibility to invest in anything allowed by law opens new avenues for business funding opportunities and increasing the odds that you will find the funding you need.

Genuine self-direction is the freedom to invest IRA & 401(k) funds as broadly as the law allows! Assets commonly held in self-directed plans include but are not limited to:

> *Promissory Notes - Closely Held Stock – LLCs – C Corporations – Startups - Real Estate - IPO Stocks - Trust Deed Notes - Oil and Gas Leases - Sales Contracts - Options – Franchises - Leases - Tax Lien Certificates – Precious Metals - Viaticals - Life Insurance (401(k) only)- Private Placement Offerings – Mortgages – LLCs*

The self-directed plan is well suited to whatever funding type you seek. I have clients who own carwashes, breeding operations, mobile home parks, windmills and other alternative assets in their self-directed plans. The options and opportunities afforded genuine self-direction are endless. There are only three things an IRA cannot buy – shares of an s-corporation, collectibles, and life insurance on the account owner. There are only two things a 401(k) cannot buy – shares in an s-corporation, and collectibles.

BE A LENDER OR FIND A LENDER

Promissory notes are a common self-directed asset. The self-directed account owner is free to prudently lend any amount of money, for a profit, to a third-party for whatever purpose including business funding on a secured or unsecured promissory note. A willing lender interested in investing retirement funds in your business has the option to open a self-directed retirement plan and lend the funds directly from the tax-protected environment of the plan. Return on investment also accumulates in the tax-protected environment of the plan. They simply:

1. Open a self-directed account;

2. Transfer all or a portion of their current retirement funds to the self-directed plan;

3. Complete the loan documents in the name of the self-directed plan;

4. Instruct plan administrator to fund the transaction and

5. Pay interest and principal payments to the retirement plan

The transfer of funds from the current retirement administrator to the self-directed administrator is not a taxable event and because the loan is executed in the name of the IRA or 401(k) and funded by the IRA or 401(k), all principal and interest is due to the plan. Therefore, all earnings accumulate in the tax-protected environment of the retirement plan. This is not a distribution; it is simply the process of purchasing a non-traditional asset within a retirement plan.

PROS FOR BUSINESS OWNERS

- Access to the trillions of dollars in IRAs and 401(k)s

PROS FOR SELF-DIRECTED ACCOUNT OWNERS

- Freedom to invest IRA/401(k) funds in anything allowed by law - the account owner is not limited to lending retirement funds to a business alone. In addition to making loans, they also have the option to invest IRA/401(k) funds in real property, precious metals, currency and other investments simultaneously.

- Assets grow in the tax-protected environment of the retirement plan

CONS FOR BUSINESS OWNERS

- You must seek investors interested in investing IRA/401(k) funds in non-traditional assets like promissory notes

- Your investors will need a self-directed IRA and/or 401(k)

- It is prohibited for the IRA/401(k) plans of you, your spouse, your ancestry, your lineal descendants and their spouses to transact business with (buy from or sell to) you or your business entities.

CONS FOR SELF-DIRECTED ACCOUNT OWNERS

- Self-direction is not well suited to everyone; if the account owner is not interested in actively participating in their IRA/401(k), self-direction may not be the right fit. Self-directed plans are well suited to individuals who take personal responsibility for their own success.

REQUIREMENTS

- Account owners interested in self-directing their IRA/401(k) must first, establish a self-directed account. Second, fund the account via cash contributions, and/or transfer of funds from existing retirement plans. Third, complete the necessary paperwork to purchase the investment using qualified professionals (i.e. legal counsel to create/review a promissory note etc.) – the paperwork must be vested in the name of the retirement plan(s) participating in the transaction. Fourth, submit the investment paperwork to the plan administrator who funds the transaction.

- When using a self-directed account, it is considered a prohibited transaction for the plan to buy from or sell to the account owner and their spouse, the account owner's ancestry (parents, grandparents...), the account owner's lineal descendants and their spouses (children, grandchildren...), and the business entities of any prohibited party. Therefore you cannot borrow from your own plan or the plan of any prohibited party. You are allowed to transact business with the plan of any willing neutral third-party. Note: brothers, sisters, aunts, uncles, cousins are not considered prohibited parties.

CLOSELY HELD STOCK

Another way to raise capital is to issue closely held stock. If the determination is made that issuing private stock is the best route for your company and its endeavor to raise capital, self-directed plans are equipped to invest. As is the case with promissory notes, the investment is made in the name of the retirement plan and funded by the plan.

If you find an investor interested in using IRA or 401(k) funds to purchase private stock in your company, they have the option to use a self-directed retirement plan to invest those funds beneath the tax-protected umbrella of the plan. They simply:

1. Open a self-directed account;

2. Transfer all or a portion of their current retirement funds to the self-directed plan;

3. Execute investment documents in the name of the self-directed plan;

4. Instruct plan administrator to fund the transaction and

5. Issue stock certificates in the name of the self-directed plan

It is considered a prohibited transaction for any prohibited party to use their retirement plan to invest in any manner in your business entities.

Pros for Business Owners

- Access to the trillions of dollars available in IRAs and 401(k)s

Pros for Self-Directed Account Owners

- Freedom to invest IRA/401(k) funds in anything allowed by law - the plan owner is not limited to purchasing closely held stock in your business alone. In addition to purchasing closely held stock they also have the option to invest IRA/401(k) funds in real property, precious metals, currency and other investments simultaneously.

- Assets grow in the tax-protected environment of the retirement plan

Cons for Business Owners

- You must seek investors interested in investing IRA/401(k) funds in closely held stock

- Your investors will need a self-directed IRA and/or 401(k)

- It is prohibited for the IRA/401(k) plans of you, your spouse, your ancestry, your lineal descendants and their spouses to transact business with (buy from or sell to) you or your business entities.

- This strategy requires competent legal counsel and thorough legal review because it may be considered a security.

Cons for Self-directed Account Owners

- Self-direction is not well suited to everyone; if the account owner is not interested in actively participating in their IRA/401(k), self-direction may not be the right fit. Self-directed plans are well suited to individuals who take personal responsibility for their own success.

REQUIREMENTS

- Account owners interested in self-directing their IRA/401(k) must first, establish a self-directed account. Second, fund the account via cash contributions, and/or transfer of funds from existing retirement plans. Third, complete the necessary paperwork to purchase the investment using qualified professionals – the paperwork must be vested in the name of the retirement plan(s) participating in the transaction. Fourth, submit the investment paperwork to the plan administrator who funds the transaction.

- When using a self-directed account, it is considered a prohibited transaction for the plan to buy from or sell to the account owner and their spouse, the account owner's ancestry (parents, grandparents...) and the account owner's lineal descendants and their spouses (children, grandchildren...), or any prohibited party's business entities. You are allowed to transact business with the plan of any willing neutral third-party. Note: brothers, sisters, aunts, uncles, cousins are not considered prohibited parties.

- Competent legal counsel – this strategy requires thorough legal review because it may be considered a security.

PARTNERSHIPS/LLCs

Self-directed plans are also capable of investing in partnerships. If you decide to make your business a partnership, self-directed retirement plans are equipped to buy ownership in your entity. If you have an interested investor, they have the option to open a self-directed retirement plan and invest funds within the tax-protected environment of the plan. They simply:

1. Open a self-directed account;

2. Transfer all or a portion of their current retirement funds to

the self-directed plan;

3. Execute Operating Agreement and Subscription documents by the plan administrator in the name of the self-directed plan and

4. Instruct the plan administrator to fund the transaction.

This strategy requires competent legal counsel to complete legal documents equipped for the retirement plan's participation. These documents are unique and specific to IRAs/401(k)s; they are not boilerplate type partnership/LLC documents.

PROS FOR BUSINESS OWNERS

- Access to the trillions of dollars available in IRAs and 401(k)s

PROS FOR SELF-DIRECTED ACCOUNT OWNERS

- Freedom to invest IRA/401(k) funds in anything allowed by law - the plan owner is not limited to partnering with your business alone. In addition to investing in the partnership they also have the option to invest IRA/401(k) funds in real property, precious metals, currency and other investments simultaneously.

- Assets grow in the tax-protected environment of the retirement plan

CONS FOR BUSINESS OWNERS

- You must seek investors interested in investing IRA/401(k) funds in a partnership

- Your investors will need a self-directed IRA and/or 401(k)

- It is prohibited for the IRA/401(k) plans of you, your spouse, your ancestry, your lineal descendants and their spouses to transact business with (buy from or sell to) you or your business entities.

Cons for Self-Directed Account Owners

- Self-direction is not well suited to everyone; if the account owner is not interested in actively participating in their IRA/401(k), self-direction may not be the right fit. Self-directed plans are well suited to individuals who take personal responsibility for their own success.

Requirements

- Plan owners interested in self-directing their IRA/401(k) must first, establish a self-directed account. Second, fund the account via cash contributions, and/or transfer of funds from existing retirement plans. Third, complete the necessary paperwork to purchase the investment using qualified professionals – the paperwork must be vested in the name of the retirement plan or retirement plans participating in the transaction. Fourth, submit the investment paperwork to the plan administrator who funds the transaction.

- When using a self-directed account, it is considered a prohibited transaction for the plan to buy from or sell to the account owner and their spouse, the account owner's ancestry (parents, grandparents...) and the account owner's lineal descendants and their spouses (children, grandchildren...), or any prohibited party's business entities. You are allowed to transact business with the plan of any willing neutral third-party. Note: brothers, sisters, aunts, uncles, cousins are not considered prohibited parties.

- Requires competent legal counsel to create the necessary legal documents. Your partnership/LLC documents must allow retirement plans to participate.

Know The Rules

In addition to knowing the freedoms afforded self-directed IRAs and 401(k)s, knowing the basic rules of the retirement plans you and/or your interested investors already have (which most likely are not self-directed plans) may be the difference between success and failure in acquiring the funding you desire. There are three tools available in most retirement plans independent of whether or not they are self-directed that may provide the business funding you need: 401(k) participant loans, IRA 60 day rollovers and 72t early retirement distributions.

401(k) Participant Loan Provision

You, your spouse, family members, and/or interested investors with 401(k), 403(b), 457, or TSP plans equipped with the participant loan provision may borrow up to 50% of the plans vested interest not to exceed $50,000 (whichever is less). This allows the account owner to borrow from their plan, for any reason (i.e. personal use, business funding, investment use, home mortgage etc.). Therefore, if your plan's vested interest is $30,000 you may borrow $15,000. If your vested interest is $50,000 you may borrow $25,000. If your vested interest is $100,000 you may borrow $50,000.

Radio and TV personalities across the country say, "Do not borrow from your 401(k)." I say whose money is it anyway? Why wouldn't you do that? The participant loan is a personal loan from your own plan that you pay back with interest at a preferential rate. The participant loan provision allows you to do more with what you already have.

For example, if we assume that you and your spouse participate in 401(k) programs through your respective employers, and that you have $125,000 vested interest, and your spouse has $75,000 vested interest, together you have the ability to borrow $87,500 FROM YOUR OWN PLANS - $50,000 from your plan, and $37,500 from your spouse's plan. This is the essence of *doing more with what you already have.*

Where else will you find this funding? If you do not have credit or collateral there is no other place to get this type of loan. And a 401(k) participant loan is not reported to the credit bureau: if you have credit card debt, a car loan etc. why wouldn't you borrow from your 401(k) plan, pay those debts down with money received at a preferential interest rate from your plan, and potentially make yourself eligible for a business loan?

If the participant loan is taken for personal use the loan is amortized over five years. If the participant loan is for a home mortgage you have 30 years to pay it back - that could free up personal money for business use instead of using it for residential or housing expenses. The key here is that this money is available to you today in the 4% range.

Whether you have a 401(k) and/or investors interested in your company have 401(k)s, the participant loan is an excellent alternative funding tool. For example, if we now assume that neither you nor your spouse participate in a 401(k) program but you have an interested investor (family, friends, third-party) who does, the investor may lend to your business using money acquired from their 401(k) participant loan. Lets assume the investor borrows $50,000 from their 401(k) to lend to your business at a 10% interest rate - you receive $50,000 at 10%, the lender pays their own 401(k) plan back at an estimated 4.25% interest rate (comparable to a 5 year CD), and the investor keeps the remaining 5.75% interest gained on the transaction personally.

The participant loan provision allows you and your potential investors to do more with what you already have. If you have a 401(k), 403(b), 457, and/or TSP plan, contact your plan administrator to inquire if the participant loan option is available through your plan.

If you are considering the participant loan option contact your tax professional to assist in determining the advisability of doing so.

Pros

- Do more with what you already have

- Borrow from your own plan at a preferential rate

- Pay your plan back with interest

- Investors may lend to you with money they acquire using their participant loan

Cons

- Not all 401(k), 403(b), 457, and TSP plan documents allow participant loans

- You must pay your plan back with interest

- The participant loan is not available in IRAs

Requirements

- Your 401(k), 403(b), 457, or TSP plan document must allow for participant loans. Contact your current plan administrator and/or request your plan's Summary Plan Description to determine whether or not your plan allows for participant loans. All plans have a Summary Plan Description. If your plan does not currently allow for this option and you are the plan sponsor, you may elect to amend your plan document to allow for participant loans or move to a 401(k) with the participant loan provision.

- You are required to pay the loan back to your plan with interest (the required interest rate is unique to each plan but in general will be somewhere around prime plus 1-2%)

- If you do not pay your plan back the loan is deemed a

taxable distribution

IRA 60-Day Rollover

Everyone says, "Don't take money out of your plan, it is dangerous." I say whose money is it anyway? There is a rule specific to IRAs (you cannot do this with a 401(k)) that allows the IRA account owner to take distribution of funds from an IRA for 60 days, use it for whatever reason without tax or penalty, as long as the sum distributed is returned to an IRA on or before the 60th day. You may do this once every 365 days per IRA account.

What would you do with this money for 60 days? People who use this strategy are often completing short-term investments. They are able to buy, sell, and put the rollover money back into the IRA on or before the 60th day. Any earnings gained on the investment are considered personal income.

For example, I have a client we will call Paul who used this strategy to pay for Christmas. Paul took distribution of $250,000 from his IRA. He bought a house that was in foreclosure. Meanwhile his friend was securing permanent financing for the house. The friend agreed to pay Paul $15,000 for temporary use of his money. Before 60 days had passed Paul returned the $250,000 to the plan, and kept the $15,000 as personal gain. When I asked Paul why he didn't complete the transaction inside his IRA and enjoy $15,000 in tax-advantaged gain, he said he planned to use the money for "Christmas cash."

Financial advisors will say, "Don't do it you might make a mistake..." (in other words "you can't count to 60"). If you are going to maximize what you already have you have to know the rules, and if you know the rules why wouldn't you use them to your benefit? This tool may provide the alternative funding you need; however you must remember it is a temporary influx of capital, and the funds must be returned to the IRA on or before the 60th day or it is considered a taxable distribution to the account owner. If the 60th day falls on a weekend or a holiday, put it back in the IRA on the 58th or 59th day - a day your administrator is doing business because a 62-day rollover will never qualify as a 60-day rollover.

Pros

- Influx of short-term capital

- Do more with what you already have

- Earnings are personal gain

- Investors may lend to you using money they acquire via 60 day rollover

Cons

- The money distributed must return to a plan on or before the 60th day

- Failure to return the money within 60 days will result in a taxable distribution

- Only available in IRAs

Requirements

- 60 days starts from the time the account owner deposits the check (the time between receipt of funds and deposit must be reasonable)

- Plan ahead - confirm your administrator is doing business the day you anticipate returning the funds

72t Early Retirement Distribution

Another tool available to both IRA and 401(k) account owners is the 72t early retirement distribution. This is the *retire when you have enough money* rule. Retirement is not some mythical, magical date that may never come. Retirement is when you have enough money. 72ts allow the account owner to take regular distributions from the retirement plan, in equal amounts every year, for either 5 years or age 59.5 (whichever is longer) and avoid the 10% premature distribution penalty assessed for taking money out of the plan before reaching 59.5 years of age.

For example, I have clients whom we will call the Smiths who retired not at age 59.5 but age 47; they retired when they had enough money. Initially the Smiths used their IRAs to purchase strip malls. Their assets created a consistent income stream for years. When their accounts reached 2.5 million this income consistency justified the Smiths' choice to set-up 72ts and start taking $15,000 distributions each month starting at age 47 and avoid the 10% early distribution penalty that would have otherwise been assessed. Eventually the Smiths stopped working and took on investing their plans full time. Their plans are now worth $5 million and they are still taking $15,000 distributions each month, penalty free.

Advisors often say "Don't do this you might make a mistake." I always question why they say that. Is it because they don't know the rules? Is it because they don't want to teach you the rules? Or are they merely thinking about the potential for lost commissions? Chances are you have an honest advisor who just doesn't know the rules or doesn't want to make a mistake. I say, whose money is it anyway? If you know the rules why wouldn't you use them to your benefit?

Pros

- Retire at any age
- Use funds received on the 72t to fund your business
- Avoid 10% premature distribution penalty

Cons

- Required to take the same amount out of the IRA each year for 5 years or until age 59.5, whichever is longer

- If at any time you cannot satisfy the 72t requirement (i.e. poor investment performance) the 10% premature distribution penalty is applied to all distributions that occurred before age 59.5

Requirements

- Must take the same amount out of the account every year for either 5 years or 59.5, whichever is longer

Conclusion

Business owners have an endless array of funding options available to them through arguably the single most accessible alternative funding source today - retirement plans. Knowing the freedoms afforded genuine self-direction, and simply knowing how to use basic IRA/401(k) rules (which are not contingent on having a self-directed plan) to your benefit provide the savvy entrepreneur unlimited access to the trillions of dollars in IRAs and 401(k)s. Knowing what IRAs and 401(k)s can really do allows you and potential investors the opportunity to do more with what you already have – this is where the money is!

~~~~~~~~~~~~~~~~~~~~~~~~~~~~~~~

Bio

Curtis L. DeYoung Founder, President, CEO, American Pension Services, Inc.®

A pioneer in the field of genuine self-direction®, Curtis L. DeYoung founded American Pension Services, Inc.® in 1982 for the purpose of allowing investors to self-direct their retirement funds as broadly as the law allows. Curtis is an active investor as well as a nationally recognized speaker and educator dedicated to teaching both independent investors, and professionals about the opportunity to invest using genuine self-direction. Curtis is an Ed Slott Master Elite Advisor with unmatched expertise in the field of genuine self-direction appearing on CNBC's Power Lunch, in the Wall Street Journal, and other financial publications.

Curtis is the Founder/former Director of the Draper Community Foundation, as well as a Director and Officer of both WaterPRO and Draper Irrigation. Curtis was the recipient of both the Draper City Citizen of the Year Award, and the Draper City Volunteer of the Year Award. Curtis is an active participant in the Boy Scouts of America organization.

American Pension Services, Inc. is a neutral third-party self-directed IRA and 401(k) administrator. Since 1982 APS® has administered retirement plans equipped to invest in anything allowed by law offering unsurpassed expertise to clients in every state. American Pension Services does not recommend, endorse, or sell investments.

American Pension Services, Inc.®
www.americanpension.com
(800) 365 6949

DISCLAIMER: The information provided herein is not intended to be relied upon as a source of investment, tax, or legal advice. While every effort has been made to present current and correct information, inadvertent errors may occur and the specific facts of each individual's situation may change the results and recommendations provided herein. While retirement plans offer nearly endless opportunities and freedoms as noted above, please realize that there are specific rules and restrictions (which may differ between different retirement plan types) regarding how retirement funds may be used to address your specific needs. In using retirement funds to acquire business funding, do not infringe on any securities laws. Please note the use of retirement funds requires the involvement of qualified professionals including the retirement plan administrator, your tax professionals, and legal counsel. Please contact your tax professionals, legal counsel and any other necessary professionals to assist in determining the advisability of involving retirement funds in your business funding endeavors.

**NOTE: THESE REQUIREMENTS
ARE SUBJECT TO CHANGE**

SECTION 4

"Don't be afraid to step outside your comfort zone on the your journey to success. You cannot make it otherwise."

~Karlene Sinclair-Robinson

SUCCEEDING ON YOUR OWN TERMS

In business, succeeding on your terms is never an easy thing to do. Finding your path to success is certainly no cake walk. Defining your level of success is important and how you get there is the scenic journey of life. But define it you must.

Wherever that journey leads you, you must be in tune with the changing tide and adjust your sails accordingly. Be susceptible to change. Be resilient. Knowing the destination is not the best part; enjoy the journey along the way.

CHAPTER 25

Core Factors for Success

There are many factors that affect us whether we become successful entrepreneurs or not. Some of these factors affect us more or less than others, as each of us has had different upbringings, approaches to life and ways of thinking. Here are a few examples of core factors that will determine whether you become a successful and rich entrepreneur or just a self-employed person.

MINDSET

Do you have the mindset to succeed as an entrepreneur? Are you willing to take the calculated risk involved with running your own business? Are you willing to give up the TV, the games, the socializing and put in the valuable time needed to nurture this new business of yours? When you think of what might be waiting for you at the end of the journey, does it make you want to fight even harder to make your business a success?

Having the right mindset is a MUST if you want to be a true entrepreneur. You cannot do this half-heartedly. It will eat you alive, one way or the other. Your mindset must be in alignment with your vision of becoming a successful entrepreneur. If your mindset focuses on the negativity and drawbacks affecting you and your business, you will not reach your true potential. Having a positive mindset can make the difference in how successful you become.

ATTITUDE

Our attitude, like our mindset, runs simultaneously on the same platform. If your attitude towards business and life is always negative, then your results will attract negative consequences. You must believe and act accordingly. If your attitude is one of positivity, then you will look at each obstacle as just part of the process or path to travel in your quest for what you desire.

The famous quote "Our Attitude Determines Our Altitude" is absolutely true. People who have a negative attitude always end up with the wrong results, while the people with a positive attitude achieve their dreams. This theory can always be tested. Start by being positive about something, and vice versa, and see what results you come away with.

VISION

Do you have THE vision? Do you see your idea or current business making a difference in your community, on the national stage, or even worldwide? Do you know what the end, or success, should look like? Have you created a vision of a successful company with the heartfelt conviction that will take you over the top? If you are lacking a vision for the new idea or current business and how it will effect change in your society, you might want to reconsider starting or staying in business.

Your vision must be in alignment with who you are. If your vision is not in alignment with you, you will not do the necessary things to make a difference. It is always important to learn about yourself, as it helps to stretch and mold you to the vision you have created. Growing into your vision will help you to manifest it bigger and better than you ever could have dreamed of.

Focus

Venturing into the entrepreneurial world takes a lot of dedication and focus. Are you focused enough to get the job done? Can you stay on task with all the things that must be done to accomplish the level of success you seek? Will you allow others to cloud your mind with reasons why you cannot do this or are you willing to put this dream of yours to the test?

When you have the focus necessary to help you deliver the results you seek, you can and will achieve some form of success. Know that what you envision might not be the exact way it plays out but know that the results are based on your focused actions that delivered. If you have to make adjustments to your original ideas, staying focused can still bring you some level of success that you can be proud of.

"One of my favorite inspirational quotes is by Maya Angelou: "I can be changed by what happens to me. I refuse to be reduced by it." What this means to me is that no matter what happens with my business or in my life's purposeful journey, I will not let it change the essence that is me. I am a child of God and He has given me my purpose...no matter the odds, I have to fulfill it. I can see it, feel it, touch it and even smell it. That's purpose!

So what's yours? What steps have you taken to pursue your purpose? There's an ancient Chinese proverb that says: "Ambition knows no obstacles." I think now is the best time to be ambitious and purposeful. Whatever you call the Divine Being, know that He has blessed you with potential, purpose - a gift. Use your faith to guide and move you towards fulfilling your purpose."

Rebekah Lynn Pierce
The GirlFriend Connection

Honesty

Often in business and life "Honesty" seems to have fallen by the wayside in our struggle, determination and climb to succeed. In allowing this essential part of our humanity to disappear, we become strangers to ourselves and others at the cost of everything and everyone else in our quest for success, money or fame. Maybe we want just success and money, or maybe we want all three. In wanting all this we somehow misplaced this vital piece of ourselves at the cost of everything else including our conscience.

Being honest is important on both a professional and a personal level. When you are dealing with a lender, you also need to be honest. Whether the lender is a banker or a private investor, being honest could possibly make your transaction work. If you lie about your situation and think that it will be okay, it is not. Remember, "Honesty is the best policy". If you lie, no one will trust you in the future. When you need the assistance of outsiders, they will not come to your aid as you cannot be trusted.

Opportunity

Is your business opportunity the right one for you? Do you believe in your gut that your idea or current business feels right, even with all the issues you have encountered or could incur? If it feels right for you, do you feel it is right for others? Is your market the right market? Is there a proven demand for your products or services? Do you have a competitive edge to offer?

> **Biz Tip:**
>
> *"Honesty is the Best Policy."*
> *When you borrow, you MUST be honest with your lender.*

This issue goes back to your business plan and what your idea or current business is about. It is important to assess these areas, as they help you define whether to move forward or get out of the kitchen.

TIMELINE

Have you given much time to what you want to do? Are you planning with proper time management or currently putting good time management to use? Do you see yourself devoting the time needed to make this business idea or current business work?

Please understand that starting a business is like having a new baby. It will take time you might not have planned for, or it might currently be eating away at what little time you have. Either way, time management is a vital piece of the puzzle in making your idea or current business a success.

IDEA

You came up with an idea for a business you feel is needed. Great! You have written down your idea and dissected it to the best of your abilities and you still feel it is applicable to your target audience. That is great but here are a few questions for you.

Is this really a viable idea to start in the current economic climate? Is the data for the new business idea credible? Is it up to date? Can your idea make a difference? Is the community going to benefit from the services or goods you will provide?

In addressing these questions, do your market research and identify your SWOT (Strengths, Weaknesses, Opportunities and Threats), which should help you determine if you are on the right path to business ownership.

RISK

The risk of starting a business and having it fail in the first year is possible. Risking everything you have to start a new business or keep the current one operational might not be the best way. On the flipside, it just might be what is needed to launch you into the stratosphere of business success. Evaluating your current situation in-depth should give you some idea as to how far to push the limits based on the future of the business you currently operate or plan to open, and the industry you are a part of. Sometimes risking everything is the key; at other times, you need to take a step back before jumping off the edge of the cliff.

On the other side of this concept of risk; you must look at the risk associated with obtaining working capital to grow your business. If your business plan model does not fit the loan you need, then the lender will not risk their money to help you. Your numbers must add up. If the current numbers and your future projections are not aligned with one another, the lender will realize that you did not effectively analyze and document them.

When you understand the lender's aversion to "RISK" or their risk tolerance, this will help you figure out what they, the lenders, are willing to finance. If the numbers do not add up and your industry type is one in trouble, this will create an issue for you. If you do not have the experience to operate such a business and you present information that is not well put together, the lender will walk away from the table.

Put yourself in the lender's shoes; would you lend to you? Seriously? Do you fit the model of an ideal borrower? When lending your own money, what interest rates would you like to earn – 2%? 5%? 10%? Think about these things before seeking "Other People's Money" (OPM). They will be more favorable to your request when you have opened your eyes to the concept of "RISK".

CHAPTER 26

Your Business as It Is Today

You might currently be operating with negative cash flow or you might only be breaking even. If so, you might not notice the new demands on your business because you are not following the changing trends or regulatory enactments. You might be too busy just trying to stay afloat and think you cannot come up for air. Being the head cook and bottle washer of your company does not leave you with enough time to keep up with much else. Effectively accomplishing the necessary changes as listed below will allow you to develop and grow your business.

1) **Business Plan** – Operating your business on the basis of a business plan that was written 5 or even 10 years ago is not acceptable. If you have not looked at the plan in a long time, then now is the time to go back to the drawing board. If you do not have a business plan, I would recommend you consider getting one done _now_. Writing a new business plan or revising an old one will get you to think about the areas in your business that are coming up short. Remember, the business plan is your road map to business success.

2) **Cash Flow Management** – Managing your business's cash flow is the life force of your business. You might think you have great products or services, but if your customers are not buying, then how great are they? Without paying customers, you are maintaining an expensive hobby. Addressing your operating expenses can also improve the net cash flow.

Review your monthly Cash Flow Projections and determine what you would like to be making over a given period of time. Then compare the projected figures to what is actually happening on a weekly or monthly basis. If the numbers are far off, then this exercise should give you some ideas as to where your business model needs adjusting.

3) **Payments** – Understanding the term "Time Value of Money" is vital. This concept affects your bottom-line. When cash is not flowing into your bank account, you cannot cover your operating expenses or increase that rainy day fund. Implementing strategies such as early pay discounts can help. With more businesses taking longer to pay their outstanding invoices, using financing options such as Factoring (the sale of your outstanding accounts receivable-invoices) can alleviate disaster and save your business. We can agree that it is better to have your money today than having to wait 30, 60, or even 90 days to get paid. Think of the ramifications of not acting quickly and no money coming in.

4) **Pricing** – This is an area where many small business owners fail. The price points of 10 years ago are not applicable today. There is an art to pricing your products and services. You must flow with the changes affecting your business. Wanting to get customers in the door by being the cheapest on the block is not necessarily the most successful way to go. Being the most expensive can also deter your growth. If your products and services cost of goods figures are too high, this will negatively impact your cash flow balance. So be sure you are pricing your products and services to meet both your needs and your customers' needs.

5) **Customer Retention** – Knowing the heart of your customers might not always be easy to figure out. Identifying ways to keep your customers coming back is important to the

longevity of your business. Use creative strategies to thank your customers, remembering important dates such as when they first became customers, their wedding anniversaries, or birthdays. If they took a long vacation consider sending them a welcome back card. Send them a handwritten "Thank You" note directly from you, stating how much you appreciate them. Doing this will make your customers feel valued and it will make you feel good in the process.

6) **Products or Services** – This is probably the most important section of all 6 topics. Why? Do you currently offer only services or just products? If you are a business owner providing only services, you had better seriously start thinking of ways to implement a product division to your business. On the other hand, the same goes for those businesses only providing products. You are losing out on sales/income by only targeting one aspect and not both. When you have multiple ways of getting paid, this just makes sense.

Remember the term, "Multiple Streams of Income"? This is how you implement and start building on your income streams. Figure out how you can improve your business cash flow and start taking the necessary actions that can make the difference between success and failure.

When considering the diversification of your business, be sure to look at your strengths, weaknesses, opportunities, and threats, (S.W.O.T.) and address them head on. Do not allow the fear of change to paralyze you from taking your small business to the next level.

CHAPTER 27

Diversifying Your Business

Here is a word for you. Diversification is the key to today's entrepreneurial success. Many entrepreneurs figure they have been successful for so long with what they are doing, they do not feel the need to make changes. How you transact business could be stifling your business's ability to have "multiple streams of income". This does not mean you have to change your business model or totally revamp everything. What you do need to do is start thinking with an "Outside of the box" cap.

Are you doing business-to-consumer (B2C), business-to-business (B2B) or business-to-government (B2G)? If you are stuck in one category, you had best start figuring out how to dissect the pie so that you can generate income through at least two of these areas.

Some entrepreneurs learned early on that diversifying their business was a key strategy to their success. Their current success hinged strongly on how well they were able to adapt and change with the shifting tide of the business world and what their clients demanded of them. Without diversification, many businesses can and will go bust.

Whom Do You Do Business With?

Your response to the above question could be the answer to your financial issues. Understanding how to maximize your client base is very important. If your business is solely concentrated on one sector, this can become a problem. Here is synopsis of who your clients are:

1. Business – to – Government = B2G

Doing business with the government can seem difficult. It can seem far-fetched for others. It is important to have this market segment as part of your business strategy for success. Not doing business with government is leaving money on the table. The U.S. government is the largest buyer of products and services in the world.

So make B2G a part of your future plans if you have not already done so. Go get the necessary certifications and invest in educational solutions that can make you a better partner for the government. Doing B2G is great when seeking non-traditional financing. Remember, it's "who's guaranteeing payments". Alternative financing sources such as Factoring sources considers this payor "A" rated, so it will help to make your access to capital much easier.

2. Business - to - Business=B2B

B2B or "Commercial" clients are also critical to a healthy balance sheet. When a business owner can segment his or her business effectively, he or she can leverage more opportunities and have a bigger reach. Doing B2B transactions will attract more alternative financing sources. Businesses are more likely to pay their bills, and so, make them a better guaranteeing source for funders.

3. Business to Consumer=B2C

Depending on how concentrated you are, if there are market trends negatively affecting this sector, you must consider how you operate your business in this market. Providing products and/or services to the consumer market is important; just understand the ups and downs that come from this sector and the ramifications it can have on your pocketbook.

Diversifying Your Business

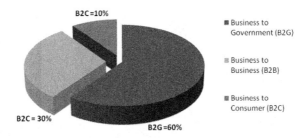

Figure 1

What do you offer?

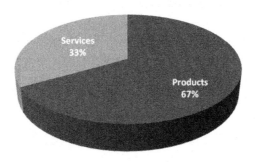

Figure 2

WHO IS GUARANTEEING PAYMENT?

When you consider diversifying your business, who is paying you is extremely important. This concept of who is guaranteed to pay their bills will better aid in accessing non-traditional forms of financing. Understanding this process will open up financing avenues that you can leverage to grow your business or help you through survival periods. Keep in mind the following order:

1) Consumer - Good

2) Business – Better

3) Government – Best

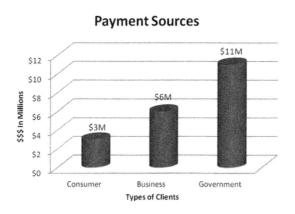

Example of Payment Sources

WHY DIVERSIFICATION IS IMPORTANT

In today's business arena, such things as personal development, consumer demands, technological and medical advancements, and many other changes are the driving forces behind the need for diversification. Without this concept of changing with the tide, many business owners will be left behind. The need to understand, and act on, what the industry advancements and the demands are, is critical. This will determine your business success or failure. Finding solutions to the growing needs of our population and economy is a vital part of how well business owners can grow their businesses.

Knowing that these changes are required, a business owner cannot allow inflexible attitudes to immobilize them. This attitude could keep them from using this concept to move their business in the direction that is being demanded of them. Understanding the strengths and weaknesses of the business model can help

Biz Tip:

Diversifying your business while staying true to the business mission will result in "Multiple Streams of Income". This is a MUST for business survival.

to impact the necessary changes. This will allow business owners to seize the opportunities presented to them based on the changing needs of the economy and their customers' buying power.

How to Implement the Concept of Diversification

Implementation of this concept is based on the business, type of industry, current economic changes, customer demands and the business owner's ability to change with the tide. Addressing each area of change is vital to this principle. Here are five (5) key areas to consider before making any changes:

1) **The Business** – Diversifying any business today can be a daunting task. How you achieve this measure of change is important but successfully achieving this change is vital. Your success is dependent on the implementation strategies set forth to move the business in the right direction. You must adapt and change or the business will not succeed or be as successful as it could be.

2) **Type of Industry** – Your industry type is important to this concept of change. Identifying the changes within your industry

will help your business if you can define a methodology to implement the changes. Take a look at the health care sector as an example. The HealthCare Reform Act of 2010 has certainly brought about many changes to how businesses within this sector operate. If they do not adapt to these changes, many businesses end up closing their doors based on compliance issues, income redistribution, and their own inability to adapt and implement these changes.

3) **Current Economic Changes** – Changes in the economy affect every business on a local, regional, national, and at times, on a global level. Just think of dropping a stone into the ocean and watching the ripple effects. These changes bring about more demands for new products or services. Sometimes these changes encourage new industries or eliminate unadaptable businesses.

4) **Customer Demands** – With the 'Baby Boomer' effects, and the coming age of the 'Echo Boomers', the demands being levied on businesses for new products and services has grown to an all time high. When a business or an industry cannot handle the demands or changes, this brings about a negative conclusion. Understanding market demands and shifts in the customer's purchasing habits will allow for growth in many sectors.

5) **Business Owner's Ability to Change** – If you are not willing to provide the products or services your clients need, they will go elsewhere. When you do not listen to your customers, they will know it. They decide where they spend their money and what they are willing to spend it on, regardless of the price point.

Diversifying your business does not mean you completely change your model. Being successful in today's market indicates that you listened to your customers and took action. If you are unable or unwilling to adapt, it will impact your bottom-line.

This is a wake-up call to those business owners who believe their customers will always buy what they have to sell. This is not the case. Start listening to your customers and implement the changes necessary to keep your business at its optimum cash flow level.

The "Why" and "How to" factors driving this need for change must be answered. It is clear that because of the ever-evolving trends in business, entrepreneurs must get on board or fail in their endeavors. Without addressing key areas of business development, the cost to your business includes losses in both your customer base and income level.

USING LEVERAGE

Leverage is a concept that can be applicable to any given situation or interaction with others. We leverage those around us to better aid the outcome of a given result that we seek. The use of leverage in business can influence many things, including income and growth. Let's use leverage in the following:

1. **Leveraging Customers** – Have them pay a percentage (e.g: 40%) prior to you providing the services or goods they require. This will help to cover upfront costs and not have you totally at risk before you get paid.

2. **Leveraging Assets** – Using such assets as real estate, equipment, accounts receivable, vehicles, or any other collateral, to gain the necessary financing you need is important. If these assets are used correctly, they can alleviate cash flow problems in the future.

3. **Leveraging Your Network** – How you leverage the people around you can help your business in a positive way. If you do not ask for assistance, no one will know what you need. This can lead to "Barter" type trade of goods and/or services that can be beneficial to those involved.

4. **The Barter Effect** – This process is back in full force. For those who have studied historical commerce or trade, you would have learned something about people using this trade practice to get what they wanted or needed. The same is still applicable today. Using barter can help startups and struggling business owners get the necessary support needed. Be sure to check out a "Barter Agreement", if necessary, as all parties would want to be on the same page when agreeing to this concept.

Be sure you understand how the concepts of leverage and diversification can work in your favor. Do not hesitate to seek out resources such as *Small Business Development Centers, S.C.O.R.E., Women's Business Centers* and many more organizations available to see you through growth or survival periods.

CHAPTER 28

Why Alternative Financing? (Non-Traditional Financing)

Many business owners could potentially qualify for bank financing. Are you one of them? Whether you have used bank financing or not, you could potentially qualify to use a variety of alternative financing options. In the event you have already pursued bank financing unsuccessfully, your ability to maximize these options can put your company on the right track to obtaining institutional financing.

REASONS FOR USING ALTERNATIVE FINANCING

There are many reasons why you might need financing. For each business owner, the need is different. Determining the best reason to seek alternative financing is one of the key strategies in the expansion of any business. Here are some reasons why you might need financial assistance:

- Business expansion

- Payroll, taxes, and/or administrative expenses

- Increase inventory/equipment

- Increase sales

- Unexpected expenses

- Fill more orders

- Pay suppliers/vendors on time

- Improvements/repairs

- Receive cash discounts for paying on time

- Extend credit to larger customers

These reasons might reflect your immediate needs or future-related expansions. Whatever your reason for seeking financing, the information here will help you get your business to the next level. It is simple: having "Cash Flow" to grow your business is a must.

ADVANTAGES OF ALTERNATIVE FINANCING

Once you, as the business owner, understand what it takes to use other people's money to grow your business, you can greatly expand your access to capital. Here are a few of the reasons to consider these options:

Growth

- Increased Production
- Increased Sales
- Take on New Orders
- Offer Cash/Volume Discounts
- Pay Suppliers on Time
- Purchase New Equipment
- Buy Real Property
- Unrestricted Use of Funds

Survival

- Meet Payroll Needs
- Pay Taxes on Time

- Meet Unexpected Expenses
- New Purchase Orders
- Contractual Obligations
- Better Credit Rating
- Improved Balance Sheet

There are many more advantages, but there is not enough room to list them all. Please understand that when you are dealing with alternative financing sources, you do not have the same amount of headaches or, should I say, strict criteria to meet when you need help.

These companies make their own decisions based on their risk evaluation and feasibility of doing such a transaction. The best part is that they will give you a fast "No" if they feel they cannot make money and/or if the risk is too much for them.

As with everything else, there are a variety of sources out there that you can tap into, so the fact that you were turned down by one alternative source does not necessarily mean that's the end of your deal. You just need to understand the market and what these companies are looking for before you actually approach them.

For example, you are looking for a commercial loan to build a development and need a certain percentage to get the project going but the banks said "No." You now have a wide array of sources throughout the country that could potentially be a good fit for your project. If time and dollars are an issue, these alternative options could be a good fit. Do some research or connect with a broker or consultant that could help you get results much faster.

If you need assistance, check with your local bank or CPA, Small Business Technical Development Centers, Women's Business

Centers, local area business consultant or broker, or S.C.O.R.E office located near you. They should be able to give you some resources based on your individual need. If all else fails, you can contact me via my website.

Must You Borrow?

It is important to consider and ask yourself this question: Do you really need to borrow other people's money (OPM)? Does your business really need the money? Do you really need to expand now? Do you really need so much money? Can you not bootstrap instead of using OPM? Think seriously about these questions.

When you chose to borrow, you put yourself and your business at risk in a number of ways. If you use traditional financing and cannot repay the loan, you stand the chance of losing whatever collateral you used to secure the financing. This could be your house, vehicles, accounts receivable, real estate or any other collateral you might have used. This could even cause you to lose your business.

I suggest you think clearly and seek to define what a "need" is and what a "want" is. Having seen many startups fail and seasoned entrepreneurs in the situation of losing everything because they overextended themselves, I caution you to take the necessary steps to borrow as little as possible.

Mixing it Up – Using Multiple Financing Options

When a business owner gets approved for a bank loan, often all their unencumbered assets are used to collateralize the loan. How about being able to use an option that does NOT use every available asset? This way of financing your business can be more attractive.

Being able to use more than one alternative financing solution during times of cash flow shortfall or expansion needs would be helpful to any business. Knowing what solutions to pick from in order to meet your financial or contractual obligations can be beneficial, to say the least.

Here are a few examples of how to use these solutions:

- **FACTORING and PURCHASE ORDER FINANCING**

  Factoring and Purchase Order Financing are two such options that can be used without one directly affecting the other. Let's say you just received a large order for products to be delivered to a "creditworthy" client (government agency). The order is for $300K. In order for you to deliver, you must pay the manufacturer or supplier $100K upfront but you do not have all of this cash available to pay them to deliver the product to your creditworthy client.

  This is where you will consider using a Purchasing Order financing source to facilitate paying the manufacturer or supplier upfront for you, so the goods can be shipped directly to your client. When the product is delivered, and your client is happy, you can then invoice them.

  In order to make this effective though, you must have a Factoring source in place also. Since you will have to wait on your client to pay their invoice, you can work with the PO funder prior to invoicing your client and the Factoring source after you have invoiced them.

- **UNSECURED LINES and More**

  If you were able to secure an Unsecured Business Line of Credit, I congratulate you. As the financing product suggests, "unsecured", you did not have to pledge any collateral to the bank to qualify for it. So, this gives you the opportunity to use almost any other option available that could benefit your business.

For instance:

- If you needed to use Factoring by selling your receivables it would not hinder your having a business line.

- If you needed to use Merchant Cash Advance, having the line would not hinder you from accessing the advance solution.

REMEMBER, in order to use any financing method, look at the collateral that is used to secure it and your current position; then follow up with the contractual fine-print in knowing what you can or cannot do.

Exit Strategies

Finally, I ask you, what exit strategies have you seriously considered if you were to receive the financing you need? When you borrow, the #1 thing the lender wants to know is this: How will they be repaid? If you cannot answer this question effectively, lending sources will not back your financing request. When the lender sees that you have a clear understanding of how you will repay them, they can then take you seriously.

Make sure you have multiple exit strategies. Some financing options will not allow you to consider this approach but others will. Be mindful of repayment timelines and the interest rates that you will have to pay. Please keep in mind that traditional financing will be the least expensive form of financing. When you have to access non-traditional or alternative financing solutions, the financing rates will be much more expensive.

Exit Options

- Increased Revenue Strategies – this can then pay off current loan and any investors.

- Refinancing – this allows for restructuring of debt, paying off current loan and investors, while allowing the borrower time to come up with a future exit strategy.

- Sell the business – selling the business at a significant profit that can then pay off any current debt is one exit strategy to seriously consider.

- Going Public – taking your business public to raise much needed capital can be a good loan/investment exit strategy, if it is the right time and avenue to take the business.

Remember, "RISK" is a factor in every lender's assessment. It does not matter what type of source you use, they all include this one little four letter word in their processing. Since non-traditional sources are taking a greater risk if they finance you, they will charge higher rates.

So, as you consider using OPM, make sure you have a clear strategy for getting out of the loan and that you understand the risks involved in using any type of outside financing.

CHAPTER 29

Documentation –
What Items Might Be Needed

All right! To get financing, you know you need to present some type of documentation. Now what? If you are contacting the financing sources for the first time, they might not ask for a lot of documentation up front. On the other hand, after you get past the initial document collection, they are going to ask for more pertinent documents.

You ask yourself, "Is it worth it to have to provide all these items?" You answer this one. If you get the money, would it be worth it? Absolutely! If not, then you certainly did not fit that particular source's requirements. Does this mean you cannot get funding? No! That's the great part. You can connect with other sources that just might be able to fund your request.

In many instances, if you have issues that might be a drawback to your receiving the funding you would like, you can write a letter explaining your position and get others to co-sign for you. This all depends, though, on what type of financing you are seeking. If you have applied to multiple sources and you keep getting the same response, you might want

> **Biz Tip:**
>
> *It is a MUST to show financial statements when borrowing OPM - Other People's Money. You will NOT be approved without them.*

to consider reviewing and/or revising your business concept, idea or plan.

Applicable Documents to Aid The Financing Process

It is important to note that when a financing source requests a particular document, you are required to provide it. If you cannot provide the document, you must have a good reason why you do not have it for them to review. Many lending sources will not consider your request if they do not receive the necessary documents to make them feel at ease in their decision to lend you their money. When they have all the documents they require, they can make the best decision on your application for funding.

Refer to Chapter 25 – Core Factors for Success under "RISK", when you review the list below.

Each financing product demands specific documentation, so do not get caught up with the list below. You will be asked for only specific documents based on the type of financing you are seeking, so let's dive right in.

Here are a few of those necessary items to get you on the road to funding:

> ## Biz Tip:
>
> *Proper documentation is necessary for all aspects of your business. Whether you are seeking financing, battling the IRS, a court case or any other situation, your records will keep you out of trouble.*

- Loan Request Summary

- Executive Summary

- Business Plan

- Articles of Incorporation and/or copy of DBA Filing

DOCUMENTATION – WHAT ITEMS MIGHT BE NEEDED

- Business License, if applicable
- Business Insurance, if applicable
- Financial Documents, e.g.:
  - Income and Expense Statement
  - Profit and Loss Statement
  - Balance Sheet
  - Cash Flow Statement
  - One to five years' Pro forma
- Use of Funds
- Federal Tax Returns
  - Personal
  - Business
- List of Debts, including pertinent details
- Accounts Receivable Aging Report
- Accounts Payable Aging Report
- Names and Contact information for all Suppliers
  - Copies of Purchase Orders
  - Sample Invoices
  - Recent Payroll Tax Form 941
  - Lease Agreements
  - Personal Financial Statement
  - Personal and Business Credit Reports

- ◦ Management Résumés

- ◦ Credit Reports for all applicable borrowers

- ◦ Equipment list, including type, age and current debt

- ◦ Copy of vendors' invoices

- ◦ Collateral Sheet

- ◦ Merchant Account Statements

- ◦ Bank Statements

- ◦ Bank References

- ◦ Voided Business Check

- ◦ Landlord Contact Information

- ◦ Photo copy of driver's licenses of primary applicants

- ◦ Proof of U.S. Citizenship

Based on the financing option that best fits your needs, a number of the items listed above would be required. Once you have submitted all the necessary paperwork, you should get a fast response regarding whether your loan has been approved or denied. In most instances, you might not have to submit too much documentation to be given a Letter of Intent or Interest, or a denial of your request.

UNDERSTAND YOUR FINANCIAL STATEMENTS

It is often noted that new business owners are not always versed in the area of all the applicable financial statements necessary to support your business. These

Biz Tip:

Do not seek financing just to pay yourself. This will kill your financing request before you even get started.

documents are not easy to understand for some, especially if in your prior career you did not have to deal with the financial aspect in order to complete your work.

With that said, you have now entered or are fully occupied in the realm of business ownership and must have some working knowledge of these necessary documents. When you analyze the data from the Small Business Administration on startup businesses referencing their success and failure rates, it is shocking to realize that many fail because they did not have a sound base, or to say it more bluntly, they did not have a clue about the financial side of their business.

Many did not understand their Cash Flow Statement and its purpose. They did not understand the significance of their Balance Sheet or even their Breakeven Point. All of these financial documents are vital to every business.

Biz Tip:

Lenders must complete "Due Diligence" before approving any loan, so be sure to give them all required documentation. No Doc, No Loan!

When a business owner understands how money flows in and out of his/her business and how to apply this process to each financial document, it will help him/her know early on if he/she is making a profit or has an expensive hobby. The IRS has a literal checklist it uses to determine whether a business is indeed a business...or an expensive hobby. Make your business financials a "must know" part of your business.

SECTION 5

"Education and its application is the key to entrepreneurial success. Without both you stand to fail as so many others have. Take your entrepreneurial education seriously and put it to work in all your business endeavors."

~Karlene Sinclair-Robinson

APPENDICES

1) Questions to Consider

2) Case Studies

3) Fraud Case Profiles

4) Recommended Reading

5) Sample Documents and Forms

6) List of Laws & IRS Publications

7) Directories

8) Web sites You Should Know

9) Business & Financing Glossary

10) About the Author

QUESTIONS TO CONSIDER

- Why do you need financing?

- Have you completed a Financial Assessment of your business?

- Is your business a viable candidate for OPM investment (Other People's Money)?

- Does the financial solution fit your business needs?

- Is the financing flexible with clear processing guidelines?

- How much financing do you really need?

- What will this financing do for your business?

- What are you looking for in a business financing partner or lender?

- Do you have to provide a Personal Guarantee?

- Are you seriously ready to access financing for your business?

- Have you already tried to obtain financing through your bank?

- What type of collateral will be needed to secure the loan?

- What if there is a default on repayment of the loan?

- What is the future of the industry you operate in?

- Does the business or you owe any government taxes?

- Can the business repay the loan?

- Can you and/or the officers of the business repay the loan in case the business fails?

CASE STUDIES

Case Study 1:

HOW ALTERNATIVE FINANCING WOULD HAVE WORKED BETTER

Case Study 2:

HOW AN ASTUTE BUSINESS OWNER USED ALTERNATIVE FINANCING

Case Study 3:

HOW HONESTY MAKES FOR THE BEST POLICY

CASE STUDY 4:

WHY UNDERSTANDING THE VALUE OF YOUR CASH FLOW IS CRITICAL

CASE STUDY 5:

WHY RELATIONSHIPS COULD BE MORE VITAL TO
YOUR BUSINESS WHEN YOU NEED A CASH INFUSION

CASE STUDY 6:

KNOWING YOUR FINANCIALS AND BEING PREPARED IS
A KEY STRATEGY TO SECURING FINANCING

CASE STUDY 7:

PAYING ATTENTION TO YOUR BUSINESS AND ITS FINANCES

CASE STUDY 8:

LEVERAGING YOUR FINANCIAL POSITION

Case Study 1:

How Alternative Financing Would Have Worked Better

The prospective client won a $1 million dollar contract and needed $19,000 to start working on the contract. It needed to purchase additional equipment and be able to pay its employees prior to its first billing cycle. The opportunity to engage this contract would put the company on the track to a level of success that many small businesses only dream of.

The prospect decided to apply for a small business loan through the Small Business Administration and was approved for $13,000 instead of the $19,000 it needed, a difference of $6,000--a huge difference. The client lost the contract because it could not come up with the $6,000 needed to start the work.

Alternative Solution

What could the prospect have done differently?

If the prospect had opted to use factoring along with equipment leasing financing, it would have been able to facilitate its $19,000 financing need. The prospect would have had access to their money ahead of its own terms. The problem, from the mouth of the client directly: "We trusted the SBA more than those other options, so we went with them." Instead, the prospect lost the contract and the company was put in a position that no small business owner should be in.

It is no longer doing business, and like many others, had to close its doors.

~~~~~~~~~~~~~~~~~

Case Study 2:

HOW AN ASTUTE BUSINESS OWNER USED ALTERNATIVE FINANCING

This prospective client contacted our financing firm seven months after receiving our marketing material. Upon interacting with the prospect through phone and e-mail and sending numerous forms of documentation, including educational materials, the prospect took another four months to come to a decision. Finally the prospect decided it was time to get moving. They were bidding on government contracts and feared that it might not be able to meet the requirements if it did not have a backup plan on how to fund its business.

ALTERNATIVE SOLUTION

After using the best financing product that was suitable for its business, factoring, for more than a year, the client won a $10 million government contract. This is huge for any small business owner considering contracting opportunities with the government. It was able to meet its payroll and other overhead obligations.

This client is now well on its way to hyper growth!

~~~~~~~~~~~~~~~~~

Case Study 3:

HOW HONESTY MAKES FOR THE BEST POLICY

When you become a potential candidate seeking alternative funding, please understand that what you did in the past can be a good thing or a major drawback.

One particular client was very smart, or so they thought. On our application, we clearly state that if there is any erroneous information because of misrepresentation, it will be cause to disqualify you from further services through our company. How can we trust and back you, if you lie to us?

The client in question chose to misrepresent the amount of taxes owed to the IRS. *Do not lie about this!* The client did state that it owed the IRS, but chose to change the figure and drop off a vital zero. We processed the application and found the client to be fair enough to take on for a factoring line. It had been a client for a few months, and then one day it won another contract, much larger —a government contract at that.

This time, the amount the client won was a little more than $1 million. With this, it needed additional working capital. Of course, from our standpoint there were no problems here; the client just needed to start working in larger business volumes.

Well, guess what! There are systems in place when you owe the IRS. The IRS found out about the contract award and decided to put a lien on the client's assets, including its accounts receivable. The accounts receivable already had a lien by the financing party, but when it comes to the IRS, the funder must take a backseat. Because the client lied and because of the amount owed, we could not and would not help the client out of that situation.

No Alternative Solution

~~~~~~~~~~~~~~~~

Case Study 4:

WHY UNDERSTANDING
THE VALUE OF YOUR CASH FLOW IS CRITICAL

A client needed to make a large purchase. The purchase would help increase the client's daily production and, of course, increase sales. The client did not want to spend its own money, even though it had the cash on hand to do so. I certainly would not want to spend my own money if I had alternatives! The client made a deposit to hold this item that would greatly help increase both its bottom and its top lines.

ALTERNATIVE SOLUTION

After contacting our financial consulting firm, we were able to facilitate the client's need through equipment lease financing. The client even had the initial deposit returned, once the transaction was approved and closing took place. The client was able to keep all its money while using the purchased item that will be owned outright at the end of the approved term.

There are huge advantages for the client, such as the fact that this type of transaction created no new debt on its balance sheet and it has tax advantages in the process (check with your CPA). Best of all, it still had its cash on hand.

Smart move!

~~~~~~~~~~~~~~~~~

Case Study 5:

WHY RELATIONSHIPS COULD BE MORE VITAL TO YOUR BUSINESS WHEN YOU NEED A CASH INFUSION

After evaluating the prospect's initial request, we considered two options that could best fit its need. These options were an unsecured business line and a merchant advance.

These two options were very well suited for the prospect, based on the type of business and the prospect's potential credit history. After a second round of processing, we determined that the only option the prospect could work with would be the merchant cash advance, so we moved forward to get the prospect the funding it needed.

During this process, the prospect was approved for a fair amount based on its cash flow and merchant advance processing volume. Everything seemed on track to getting the prospect what it was looking for. As part of a merchant advance processing, the business owner's landlord must be contacted to validate the information provided to us and to determine the relationship between the business owner and landlord. The length of your lease in this type of financing transaction is vital.

When the landlord finally responded, we discovered that the prospect had a very bad relationship with the landlord. To make things worse, the landlord was not planning to renew the lease agreement, and the lease was close to the end of its term.

This information immediately changed the dynamics of the request. The business owner could not show that it had a renewed lease with either the current landlord or a new one, so the funder decided that the candidate was too great a risk. If the prospect did not have a contracted commercial location in which to do business for at least another year, then the funder might have a problem getting compensated, if it was to loan money to the prospect. Because of the negative relationship with the landlord, the prospect was unable to get the cash infusion the company needed.

ALTERNATIVE SOLUTION

NONE, except be honest upfront and DO NOT waste people's time.

~~~~~~~~~~~~~~~~~

Case Study 6:

KNOWING YOUR FINANCIALS AND BEING PREPARED IS A KEY STRATEGY TO SECURING FINANCING

When a business owner is forced to seek outside financing, it is important that they know their financial documents well enough. This particular business owner had been in business for four years providing contractual services to governmental agencies and other small businesses. It is important to note that I am not sure how this company was able to win a government contact based on the business owner's inadequate knowledge of financial statements.

During the time that he was seeking a capital infusion, the basic paperwork that was needed, such as balance sheet and cash flow statements could not be provided because he did not know what those were, nor did he know how to fill them out. In trying to work with this potential client, assisting him with the paperwork was one thing; having some form of decent records to show his invoicing, income and expenses, proved futile. The financing source went as far as to visit with this business owner face-to-face just to see if this could be as bad as it sounded. It was.

To make matters worse, the initial invoice that was presented as part of the financing request showed some discrepancies, so we requested a second one. The second invoice proved what we realized: the business owner had made the colossal mistake. One invoice recorded that the bill was to be paid to the owner in his name and on the second invoice it had the correction: paid to company name.

With all of the above issues, no financing source would be willing to fund such an ill-prepared candidate.

ALTERNATIVE SOLUTION

None from a financing aspect. They were advised to get technical business development training immediately.

~~~~~~~~~~~~~~~~~

Case Study 7:

PAYING ATTENTION TO YOUR BUSINESS
AND ITS FINANCES

It is great to have good staff. It is also important to pay attention to your business and not leave everything up to employees. With that said, giving personnel the freedom to work is not a bad idea but you must do your part to monitor your financials, income and expenditures, etc., as you are responsible for the actions of your company, to a certain extent.

In this case, the business owner felt everything was going so well, she did not have to keep up with the internal operations of the business. Unfortunately, whether it is greed, power or out of necessity, employee fraud occurs more frequently than you can imagine. This was the case. The employee in this healthcare organization figured she could not get caught and defrauded both the company,

Medicare and Medicaid to the tune of hundreds of thousands of dollars. This all happened right under the business owner's nose due to her lack of involvement on many levels and giving this one individual too much authority with no oversight.

The outcome came when the company started losing money; the business owner realizing what was going on and ended up having to call in the FBI on her own employee. Due to this employee's actions, it caused a lot of trauma and headache for many. This brought the business to a halt financially. In the long run, it could not sustain the downward spiral and eventually had to close its doors.

ALTERNATIVE SOLUTION

Business owners must pay attention to their businesses, especially their financial positions. This will help them identify problems early on and keep them out of trouble in the long run.

~~~~~~~~~~~~~~~~~~

Case Study 8:

LEVERAGING YOUR FINANCIAL POSITION

Operating a successful business today can be a daunting task. With that said, it can be done. This is the story one such success business owner who did so on their terms. Starting up a business in a highly regulated industry can take its toll on anyone. The business in question had to provide documentation showing financial positions at a certain level. This information had to be presented to the department seeking said information on an ongoing basis in order to qualify to bill the government for services rendered.

After a very lengthy process, the business owner finally met all the criteria that had been put in place. How did they do this? By using up every penny in their Home Equity Line of Credit, personal credit lines, cashing out their retirement accounts and additional capital investments, not to mention the initial investment they had saved up prior to starting the business.

ALTERNATIVE SOLUTIONS: The business owner, based on his credit, could have qualified for both an unsecured business and personal credit lines but was unwilling to try those financing methodologies. He qualified for the line, but did not accept it. Lucky for him, he was able to sustain the business, just barely, to get the approval he needed.

~~~~~~~~~~~~~~~~~

Case Study 9:

TEAMWORK IS VITAL TO YOUR FINANCING CAPABILITIES

Knowing that your business could be in jeopardy if you cannot access additional financing can cause a lot of nightmares. When this particular business owner needed additional capital, she had already received an SBA Guaranteed loan from a local lender not even 18 months prior. She did not know what to do but doing nothing would have caused her to lose the new contract she had just won.

When she had received the initial loan, her Accounts Receivable and other assets were used as collateral in securing the loan, so she could not immediately see a way around her going forward. This is where teamwork is a must in helping businesses stay open. Finding solutions to daily situations is important and that is how we get to tell the stories.

ALTERNATIVE SOLUTION: The SBA lender, the business owner and an alternative financing source were able to work out a solution that was amicable to all parties. This workout was certainly based on the individual situation and the willingness of all involved to make it work.

PS... This does not work in all cases.

FRAUD CASE
PROFILES

FRAUD CASE PROFILED
Former Finance Executive of New Jersey Company Pleads Guilty to Wire Fraud, Money Laundering, and Tax Fraud

CAMDEN, NJ November 17, 2011 - Rusty Spickenreuther, 46, of Franklinville, N.J., The former controller of an environmental and industrial services firm based in Swedesboro, N.J., admitted to defrauding his former employer by improperly diverting funds and taking more than $1.3 million from the company Spickenreuther admitted that between June 2009 and June 2011, he embezzled from his former employer, Environmental Industrial Services Corp. of New Jersey, by stealing more than 50 checks payable to the company and diverting the funds to bank accounts he controlled. Spickenreuther deposited the checks—which ranged from $255 to more than $88,000—into a bank account he set up in the name of "EISCO," an acronym that is regularly used to refer to the company.

For the 2009 and 2011 tax years, Spickenreuther did not disclose to the IRS the income that he received in connection with the fraudulent scheme. Spickenreuther failed to disclose in excess of $760,000, resulting in a tax loss to the United States of $258,712. As part of his guilty plea, Spickenreuther has agreed to make full restitution to the victims of his offenses for all losses resulting from his crime.

The wire fraud charge carries a maximum potential penalty of 20 years in prison and a $250,000 fine or twice the pecuniary gain or loss resulting from Spickenreuther's criminal conduct. The money laundering charge carries a maximum potential penalty of 10 years in prison and a $250,000 fine or twice the pecuniary gain or loss resulting from Spickenreuther's criminal conduct. The tax fraud charges carry a maximum potential penalty of three years in prison and a $100,000 fine. Sentencing is scheduled for Feb. 27, 2012.

Source: http://www.fbi.gov/news

FRAUD CASE PROFILED
Yuma Donut Shop Owner Pleads Guilty to Making
False Representations and to Failing to Pay Overtime

August 24, 2011 PHOENIX—TONG—Seng Jerry Luy, 45, of Yuma, Ariz., pleaded guilty on August 23, 2011, in federal court in Phoenix to concealment by trick and to willful failure to pay overtime. The case arises out of an earlier civil investigation by the U.S. Department of Labor into the employment practices at Luy's Yuma restaurant, Arizona Donut & Café. "Our partners at the Department of Labor and the FBI went the extra mile, as they always do, to seek justice for employees who were exploited," said U.S. Attorney Dennis K. Burke. "This employer took extraordinary measures to avoid paying low-wage workers their rightful overtime wages under the law," said Eric Murray, district director of the Wage and Hour Division's Phoenix office.

In his plea agreement, Luy admitted he knew the law required him to pay overtime wages (an additional one half of the hourly rate of pay) to his employees when they worked in excess of 40 hours in a work week, but that he did not do so. He further admitted that he discussed the law with Department of Labor representatives who were investigating his business between July and September 2010, that he agreed with the Department of Labor that he owed over $27,000 in past-due overtime wages to eight employees, and that he would pay those wages by October 31, 2010. In lieu of paying the past-due wages, he printed repayment checks, required his employees to endorse those checks back over to him, and presented the fronts of the checks to the Department of Labor to make it seem as though he had repaid his employees pursuant to the agreement. Luy also admitted that he continued to fail to pay overtime to his employees for new work following his agreement with the Department of Labor.

A conviction for concealment by trick carries a maximum penalty of five years in federal prison, a $250,000 fine, or both. A conviction for willful failure to pay overtime carries a maximum penalty of six months in federal prison, a $10,000 fine, or both.

Source: http://www.fbi.gov/news

FRAUD CASE PROFILED
South Carolina Man Pleads Guilty to Receipt of
Commissions or Gifts in Procuring Loans

October 28, 2011 COLUMBIA, SC—United States Attorney Bill Nettles stated today that Matthew Skinner, age 36, of Pawley's Island, South Carolina, pled guilty today in federal court in Florence, to receipt of commissions or gifts for procuring loans, a violation of Title 18, United States Code, Section 215. Evidence presented at the guilty plea hearing established that Mr. Skinner had been an employee of RBC Bank (USA), and that on June 20, 2008, in Horry County, Mr. Skinner accepted payment from a private individual not associated with the bank in connection with mortgage loans. Mr. Skinner also admitted to accepting payments on several other occasions.

Mr. Nettles stated the maximum penalty Skinner can receive is a fine of $1,000,000 and/or imprisonment for 30 years, plus a special assessment of $100. The case was investigated by agents of the Federal Bureau of Investigation. Assistant United States Attorney John C. Potterfield of the Columbia office handled the case.

Source: http://www.fbi.gov/news

FRAUD CASE PROFILED
Owner of Brunsman Companies Sentenced to
12 Years in Prison for $50 Million Fraud

September 22, 2011 CINCINNATI—Richard T. Brunsman Jr., 45, of Cincinnati was sentenced in United States District Court to 144 months in prison for fraudulently obtaining more than $62 million in loans from 18 different federally insured banks for his companies. Brunsman was ordered to repay the banks $49,742,343.16 in restitution, which represents the amount they lost.

Brunsman applied for the loans between 2004 and 2010 claiming the money would be used for one or more of the approximately 20 solely owned businesses he had. He created numerous false documents including false financial statements and other documents for his companies in order to obtain the loans.

Analysis of his bank records during the investigation found that he used the money he fraudulently obtained to live an expensive lifestyle that included a large house in Cincinnati, a waterfront condo in Florida, and a large yacht. He took numerous trips, including trips to California and Las Vegas, and enjoyed entertaining.

Brunsman became engaged in so many businesses, real estate purchases, and other investments that he lost significant funds in these ventures. When banks expressed concern about signs of fraud in the loans, Brunsman responded by fraudulently obtaining more loans from other lenders to pay off the loans at the banks that were asking questions.

He pleaded guilty on February 22, 2011 to one count of bank fraud.

"In the end, the Defendant left an unparalleled trail of devastation through the Cincinnati banking community," Assistant U.S. Attorney Timothy Mangan wrote in a sentencing memorandum filed with the court.

Brunsman's sentence includes an order that he forfeit all fraud-related assets which are proceeds of the crime. Judge Dlott ordered Brunsman to report to the Bureau of Prisons on November 28, 2011 to begin serving his sentence.

Source: http://www.fbi.gov/news

FRAUD CASE PROFILED
Loan Brokerage Company, Its Owners, and an Associate
Indicted for Alleged $37 Million Bank Fraud Conspiracy

November 17th, 2011 BALTIMORE—A federal grand jury has indicted Jade Capital & Investments, LLC, and its owners, brothers Joon Park, a/k/a "Joon Pak," and "Joon Paik," age 41, of Falls Church, Virginia, and Loren Young Park, a/k/a "Loren Yong Park," and "Yong Park," age 44, of Vienna, Virginia, on charges connected to a scheme to fraudulently obtain business loans guaranteed by the Small Business Administration, with resulting losses alleged to be over $37 million. Nick Park, a/k/a Nochol Park, age 46, of McLean, Virginia, an associate of Joon and Loren Park, but no relation, was also charged in the scheme. The indictment was returned on November 8, 2012 and unsealed today...

According to the nine count indictment, Jade Capital was a loan brokerage company operated by Joon and Loren Park and specializing in securing loans for individuals interested in purchasing or refinancing small businesses in the Mid-Atlantic area...

The indictment alleges that from February 2005 until October 2011, Joon, Loren, and Nick Park submitted SBA loan applications and supporting documentation to loan originators and underwriters on behalf of their clients. The indictment alleges that the packages contained fraudulent personal financial statements and/or monthly bank statements which overstated the net worth and equity injection of the borrowers and falsely enhanced the creditworthiness of the borrowers and their businesses...

The defendants face a maximum sentence of 30 years in prison for the bank fraud conspiracy and for each count of bank fraud.

An indictment is not a finding of guilt. An individual charged by indictment is presumed innocent unless and until proven guilty at some later criminal proceedings...

Source: http://www.fbi.gov/news

RECOMMENDED READING

*"A person who won't read has no advantage
over one who can't read." Mark Twain*

1. Aspire – Kevin Hall
2. Attitude is Everything – Keith Harrell
3. Become Your Own Boss in 12 Months – Melinda Emerson
4. Book Yourself Solid – Michael Port
5. Cash Flow for Dummies – Tage C. Tracy and John A. Tracy
6. Endless Referrals, Third Edition – Bob Burg
7. Escape from Cubicle Nation – Pamela Slim
8. Financial Intelligence for Entrepreneurs – Karen Berman & Joe Knight
9. Flash Foresight – Daniel Burrus with John David Mann
10. Get Your Business Funded – Steven D. Strauss
11. Go For No! – Richard Fenton & Andrea Waltz
12. Guerilla Marketing for Small Businesses – Jay Conrad Levinson
13. How to Build Buzz for Your Biz – Wendy Kenney
14. How to Win Friends and Influence People – Dale Carnegie
15. If Nobody Loves You Create the Demand – Joel A. Freeman
16. It's Not About You - Bob Burg and John David Mann
17. Lawyers are Liars – Mark Kohler
18. Making the Jump into Small Business – David Nilssen and Jeff Levy
19. Mindset – Carol Dweck
20. One Simple Idea – Stephen Key
21. Own Your Niche – Stephanie Chandler

22. People Buy You – Jeb Blount

23. Pricing with Confidence – Reed Holden and Mark Burton

24. Raising Venture Capital for the Serious Entrepreneur – Dermot Berkery

25. Reading Financial Reports for Dummies – Lita Epstein, MBA

26. Seizing the White Space – Mark W. Johnson

27. Startup Smarts – Barry H. Cohen & Michael Rybarski

28. Steve Jobs - Walter Isaacson

29. The Art of The Start – Guy Kawasaki

30. The Collaborator Rules – Sally Shields

31. The E-Myth Revisited – Michael E. Gerber

32. The Enthusiastic Networker – Juli Monroe

33. The Entrepreneur Equation – Carol Roth

34. The Go-Giver – Bob Burg & John David Mann

35. The Lean Startup – Eric Ries

36. The Personal MBA: Master the Art of Business – Josh Kaufman

37. The Power of Now – Eckhart Tolle

38. The Richest Man In Babylon – George S. Clason

39. The Rules of Money – Robert Templar

40. The SBA Loan Book – Charles H. Green

41. The Toilet Paper Entrepreneur – Mike Michalowicz

42. Think and Grow Rich – Napoleon Hill

43. Use What You Have To Get What You Want – Jack Nadel

44. You Are What You Think – David Stoop, Ph.D.

SAMPLE DOCUMENTS
& FORMS

SBA COLLATERAL CHECKLIST

COLLATERAL TYPE	LENDER	SBA
House	Market Value x 0.75 - Mortgage balance	Market Value x 0.80 - Mortgage balance
Car	Not applicable	Not applicable
Truck & Heavy Equipment	Depreciated Value x 0.50	Same
Office Equipment	Not applicable	Not applicable
Furniture & Fixtures	Depreciated Value x 0.50	Same
Inventory: Perishables	Not applicable	Not applicable
Jewelry	Not applicable	Not applicable
Other	10%-50%	10%-50%
Receivables	Under 90 days x 0.75	Under 90 days x 0.50
Stocks & Bonds	50%-90%	50%-90%
Mutual Funds	Not applicable	Not applicable
Individual Retirement Account (IRA)	Not applicable	Not applicable
Certificate of Deposit (CD)	100%	100%

S.W.O.T ANALYSIS

Complete each section to help you define your best business model or changes to your current business. You should also consider completing an analysis of your personal strengths and weaknesses.

STRENGTHS	WEAKNESSES
1)	1)
2)	2)
3)	3)
4)	4)
OPPORTUNITIES	**THREATS**
1)	1)
2)	2)
3)	3)
4)	4)

ALTERNATIVE FINANCING
EVALUATION

	Self/ Family	Peer-to-Peer	Cash Advance	AR Financing / Factoring	Bank/Debt Financing	Asset Financing	Venture Capital	Crowd Funding
Unlimited								
Cost efficient								
Nothing to pay back								
No debt on balance sheet								
Debt capacity unchanged								
No cost when Unused								
No restrictions on use of money								
No intrusion into service operations								
No personal guarantee								
Limited collateral								
Simple to apply and acquire								
Applicant's creditworthiness unimportant								
Ability to manage cost								

PRO FORMA
CASH FLOW SAMPLE

	2012	2013	2014	2015	2016
Cash Received					
Cash from Operations					
Cash Sales					
Cash from Receivables					
Subtotal Cash from Operations					
Additional Cash Received					
Sales Tax, VAT, HST/GST Received					
New Current Borrowing					
New Other Liabilities (interest-free)					
New Long-term Liabilities					
Sales of Other Current Assets					
Sales of Long-term Assets					
New Investment Received					
Subtotal Cash Received					
EXPENDITURES					
Expenditures from Operations					
Cash spending					
Bill Payments					
Subtotal Spent on Operations					
Additional Cash Spent					
Sales Tax, VAT, HST/GST Paid Out					
Principal Repayment of Current Borrowing					
Other Liabilities Principal Repayment					

Long-term Liabilities Principal Repayment					
Purchase Other Current Assets					
Purchase Long-term Assets					
Dividends					
Subtotal Cash Spent					
Net Cash Flow					
Cash Balance					

PRO FORMA PROFIT AND LOSS TEMPLATE

	2012	2013	2014	2015	2016
SALES					
Direct Costs of Goods					
Other Production Expenses					
COST OF GOODS SOLD					
Gross Margin					
Gross Margin %					
EXPENSES					
Payroll					
Sales and Marketing and Other Expenses					
Depreciation					
Meals and Entertainment					
Licenses, Permits & Fees					
Travel Expense					
Rent					
Utilities					
Supplies					
Telephone					
Postage and Delivery					
Consulting Fees					
Legal and Professional					
Employee Training					
Insurance and Bonding					
Payroll Taxes					
Other					
Other					
Total Operating Expenses					
Profit Before Interest and Taxes					
Interest Expense					
Taxes Incurred					
Net Profit					
Net Profit/Sales					

ACCOUNTS RECEIVABLE
AGING REPORT SAMPLE

Creditor	Date	Last Payment Amount	Current 0-30	31-60	61-90	Past Due 91-119	120-150	150+	Total Due
Customer	02/02/12	$25,300	$11,810	$3,420	$1,005				$16,235
Customer	02/08/12	$8,910	$1,550	$6,745	$1,879	$1,665		$3,243	$15,082
Customer	12/19/11	$15,035	$530	$1,874	$1,675		$1,606		$5,685
Customer	01/21/12	$6,550	$3,365	$16,040	$1,160				$20,565
		Totals	$17,255	$28,079	$5,719	$1,665	$1,606	$3,243	$57,567

ACCOUNTS PAYABLE AGING
REPORT SAMPLE

		Last Payment		Current		Past Due			
Creditor	Date	Amount	0-30	31-60	61-90	91-119	120-150	150+	Total Due
Supplier	02/02/12	$25,300	$11,810	$3,420	$1,005				$16,235
Supplier	02/08/12	$8,910	$1,550	$6,745	$1,879	$1,665		$3,243	$15,082
Supplier	12/19/11	$15,035	$530	$1,874	$1,675		$1,606		$5,685
Supplier	01/21/12	$6,550	$3,365	$16,040	$1,160				$20,565
		Totals	$17,255	$28,079	$5,719	$1,665	$1,606	$3,243	$57,567

BALANCE SHEET SAMPLE

As of _____/_____/_____

ASSETS

Current Assets

Cash Available	_____
Accounts Receivable	_____
(less doubtful accounts)	_____
Inventory	_____
Temporary Investment	_____
Prepaid Expenses	_____
Total Current Assets	_____

Fixed Assets

Long-term investments	_____
Land	_____
Buildings	_____
(less accumulated depreciation)	_____
Plant and Equipment	_____
(less accumulated depreciation)	_____
Furniture and fixtures	_____
(less accumulated depreciation)	_____
Total Net Fixed Assets	_____

LIABILITIES

Current Liabilities

Accounts Payable	_____
Short-term notes	_____
Current portion of long-term notes	
Interest Payable	_____
Taxes Payable	_____
Accrued Payroll	_____
Total Current Liabilities	_____

Long-term Liabilities

Mortgage	_____
Other long-term liabilities	_____
Total Long-Term Liabilities	_____

Shareholders' Equity

Capital Stock	_____
Retained Earnings	_____
Total Shareholders' Equity	_____

TOTAL ASSETS _____   TOTAL LIABILITIES & EQUITY _____

255

CASH FLOW STATEMENT SAMPLE

| Company Name | | | MONTH BY MONTH CASH FLOW | | | | | | | | | | YR: | 2012 |

MONTH		JAN	FEB	MAR	APR	MAY	JUN	JUL	AUG	SEP	OCT	NOV	DEC	TOTAL
SALES	Product or Services Income													0
Less:	Costs of Goods Sold													0
GROSS PROFIT		0	0	0	0	0	0	0	0	0	0	0	0	0
EXPENSES	Officers Salary													0
Less:	Staff Salary													0
	Payroll Taxes													0
	Office Supplies													0
	Building Rent / Mortgage Pymt													0
	Equipment Rental													0
	Repairs													0
	Insurance													0
	Bank Charges													0
	Vehicle Expenses													0
	Utilities													0
	Telephone													0
	Professional Fees													0
	Contracted Labor													0
	Dues & Subscriptions													0
	Advertising													0
	License & Taxes													0
	Depreciation & Amortization													0
	Lease Payments													0
	Interest Expense													0
	Other Expenses ____ Name													0
	Other Expenses ____ Name													0
	Other Expenses ____ Name													0
Less:	TOTAL EXPENSES	0	0	0	0	0	0	0	0	0	0	0	0	0
NET PROFIT		0	0	0	0	0	0	0	0	0	0	0	0	0
Less:	Owners' Withdrawals													
AMOUNT AVAILABLE FOR LOAN		0	0	0	0	0	0	0	0	0	0	0	0	0
Less:	Loan Principal Payment													
BALANCE RETAINED BY BUSINESS		0	0	0	0	0	0	0	0	0	0	0	0	0

LIST OF LABOR LAWS
AND
IRS PUBLICATIONS

LIST OF LABOR LAWS

The following is a list of Federal laws that business owners with employees must comply with. Check the Department of Labor's website for more information at http://www.dol.gov:

1. ADA-Americans with Disabilities Act (1990) *(14 employees or more)*

2. ADEA-Age Discrimination in Employment Act (1967) *(19 employees or more)*

3. EPA -Equal Pay Act (1963) (applicable to all)

4. FICA-Federal Insurance Contribution Act (1930s) *(applicable to all)*

5. FLSA-Fair Labor Standards Act (1938) *(applicable to all)*

6. FUTA-Federal Unemployment Tax Act (1935) *(applicable to all)*

7. IRCA-Immigration Reform and Control Act (1986)*(applicable to all)*

8. Medicare *(applicable to all)*

9. OSHA-Occupational Safety and Health Administration Act (1970)*(10 employees or more)*

10. Pregnancy Discrimination Act (1978) *(14 employees or more)*

11. Social Security (1935) *(applicable to all)*

12. Title VII Civil Rights Act (1964)

IRS PUBLICATIONS FOR BUSINESSES

Publication	Description
Publication 15	Publication 15, (Circular E), Employer's Tax Guide
Publication 334	Tax Guide for Small Business (For Individuals Who Use Schedule C or C-EZ)
Publication 463	Travel, Entertainment, Gift, and Car Expenses
Publication 505	Tax Withholding and Estimated Tax
Publication 531	Reporting Tip Income
Publication 535	Business Expenses
Publication 547	Casualties, Disasters, and Thefts (Business and Non-business)
Publication 560	Retirement Plans for Small Business (SEP, SIMPLE, and Qualified Plans)
Publication 583	Starting a Business and Keeping Records
Publication 587	Business Use of Your Home (Including Use by Day-Care Providers)
Publication 598	Tax on Unrelated Business Income of Exempt Organizations
Publication 946	How to Depreciate Property
Publication 1635	Understanding Your EIN - Employer Identification Numbers. This publication is designed to educate the public about the Employer Identification Number (EIN). It explains what an EIN is, how to know if you need one for your business and provides application criteria.
Publication 1779	Independent Contractor or Employee

RECORD KEEPING IN YEARS

1. Accounts Payable Ledgers	10 years
2. Accounts Receivable Ledgers	10 years
3. Audit Reports	Permanently
4. Bank Statements	3 years
5. Business Tax Returns	Permanently
6. Business Financial Records	Permanently
7. Contracts, Mortgages, Notes and Leases (expired)	10 years
8. Copyrights	Permanently
9. Deeds, Mortgages,	Permanently
10. Patents and related documents	Permanently
11. Payroll Records and Summaries	10 years
12. Personnel Files (terminated)	10 years
13. Petty Cash Vouchers	3 years
14. Property Records including blueprints, depreciation schedule	Permanently
15. Retirement and Pension Records	Permanently
16. Sales Commission reports	3 years

17. Sales Records	10 years
18. Time books/Sheets/Cards	10 years
19. Trademark Registrations	Permanently
20. Withholding Tax Statements	10 years

APPLICABLE TAX FORMS

IF you are a...	THEN you may be liable for...	Use Form...
Sole proprietor	Income tax	1040 and Schedule C [1] or C-EZ (Schedule F [1] for farm business)
	Self-employment tax	1040 and Schedule SE
	Estimated tax	1040-ES
	Employment taxes:	
	Social security and Medicare taxes and income tax withholding	941 (943 for farm employees)
	Federal unemployment (FUTA) tax	940
	Depositing employment taxes	8109 [2]
	Excise taxes	See *Excise Taxes*
Partnership	Annual return of income	1065
	Employment taxes	Same as sole proprietor
	Excise taxes	See *Excise Taxes*
Partner in a partnership (individual)	Income tax	1040 and Schedule E [3]
	Self-employment tax	1040 and Schedule SE
	Estimated tax	1040-ES

Corporation or S corporation	Income tax	1120 or 1120-A (corporation) [3] 1120S (S corporation) [3]
	Estimated tax	1120-W (corporation only) and 8109 [2]
	Employment taxes	Same as sole proprietor
	Excise taxes	See *Excise Taxes*
S corporation shareholder	Income tax	1040 and Schedule E [3]
	Estimated tax	1040-ES

Source: *Internal Revenue Service (IRS) www.irs.gov*

DIRECTORIES

GOVERNMENT

Bureau of Economic Analysis
Survey of Current Business -- monthly report
1441 L Street, NW, Washington, DC 20230
Phone (Public Information Office): 202-606-9900
Phone (Gross Domestic Product): 202-606-9732
(Virginia Mannering)
http://www.bea.gov

Bureau of Labor Statistics (BLS)
2 Massachusetts Avenue, NE, Washington, DC 20212-0001
Phone (Labor force concepts): 202-691-6378
Phone (Information specialists): 202-691-5200
(recorded messages)
http://www.bls.gov

Federal Depository Libraries
http://www.gpoaccess.gov/libraries.html

Minority Business Development Agency (MBDA)
U.S. Department of Commerce
1401 Constitution Avenue, NW, Washington, DC 20230
Toll-free: 1-888-324-1551
http://www.mbda.gov

National Women's Business Council (NWBC)
409 Third Street, SW, Suite 210, Washington, DC 20024
Phone: 202-205-3850 / Fax: 202-205-6825
http://www.nwbc.gov

Office of Women's Business Ownership
Small Business Administration (SBA)
409 Third Street, SW, 4th Floor, Washington, DC 20416
Phone: 202-205-6673
http://www.sba.gov

Office of Government Contracting and Business Development (GCBD)
Assistance for Women Business Owners
409 Third Street, SW, 8th Floor, Washington, DC 20416
Phone: 202-205-7315
http://www.sbaonline.sba.gov/aboutsba/sbaprograms/gcbd/in-dex.html

Small Business Administration (SBA)
Dept. P, 409 Third St., SW, Washington, DC 20416
Toll-free: 1-800-827-5722
http://www.sba.gov

U.S. Department of Veteran Affairs (VA)
The Center for Veterans Enterprise (VACVE)
810 Vermont Avenue, NW, Washington, DC 20420
Phone: 202-303-3260 / Toll-free: 1-866-584-2344
Fax: 202-254-0238
http://www.vetbiz.gov

Women's Bureau - Department of Labor
200 Constitution Avenue, NW, Room S-3002, Washington, DC 20210
Phone: 202-693-6769 / Fax: 202-693-6776
http://www.dol.gov/wb/

ORGANIZATIONS AND ASSOCIATIONS

American Association of Franchises and Dealers
P.O. Box 81887, San Diego, CA 92138-1887
Toll-free: 1-800-733-9858 / Fax: 619-209-3777
http://www.aafd.org

American Bankers Association
1120 Connecticut Avenue, N.W., Washington, DC 20036
Phone: 1-800-BANKERS
http://www.aba.com

American Business Women's Association
11050 Roe Ave., Suite 200, Overland Park KS. 66211
Phone: 1-800-228-0007
http://www.abwa.org

Asian American Business Development Center
80 Wall Street, Suite 148, New York, NY 10005
Phone: 212-966-0100 / Fax: 212-966-2786
http://www.aabdc.com/aabdc_upload/newhome.php

Center for Women's Business Research
1760 Old Meadow Road, Suite 500, McLean, VA 22102
Phone: 703-556-7162 / Fax: 703-506-3266
http://www.womensbusinessresearch.org

Count Me In for Women's Economic Independence
240 Central Park South, Suite & 7GH
New York, New York 10019
Phone: (212) 245-1245 / Fax: (212) 245-1236
http://www.makemineamillion.org
http://www.countmein.org

Directory of African American Businesses
1913 Marion Street, Suite 202, Columbia, SC 29201
Phone: 803-254-6404 / Toll-free: 1-800-419-2417
Fax: 301-229-6133
http://blackpagesusaonline.com

Entrepreneurs' Organization – Global Headquarters
500 Montgomery Street, Suite 700
Alexandria, VA 22314 USA
Phone: 703-519-6700 / Fax: 703-519-1864
http://www.eonetwork.org

Family Firm Institute, Inc.
200 Lincoln Street, #201, Boston, MA 02111
Phone: 617-482-3045 / Fax: 617-482-3049
http://www.ffi.org

International Franchise Association (IFA)
1501 K Street, NW, Suite 350, Washington, DC 20005
Phone: 202-628-8000 / Fax: 202-628-0812
http://www.franchise.org

Joint Center for Political and Economic Studies
1090 Vermont Ave., NW, Suite 1100,
Washington, DC 20005-4928
Phone: 202-789-3500 / Fax: 202-789-6390
http://www.jointcenter.org

My Own Business Inc.
13181 Crossroads Parkway North, Suite 190,
City of Industry, CA 91746
Phone: 562-463-1800 / Fax 562-463-1802)
http://www.myownbusiness.org

National Association of Minority Contractors
Washington, DC Metropolitan Area Chapter
2307 Skyland Place, SE, Suite A, Washington, DC 20020
Phone: 202-678-8840 / Fax: 202-678-8842
http://www.namcdc.net

National Association of Professional Employer Organizations
707 North Saint Asaph St., Alexandria, VA 22314
Phone: 703-836-0466 / Fax: 703-836-0976
http://www.napeo.org

National Association of Women Business Owners (NAWBO)
601 Pennsylvania Avenue NW, South Building, Suite 900
Washington, DC 20004
Tel: 1-800-556-2926 / Fax: 202-403-3788
http://www.nawbo.org

National Black Chamber of Commerce
1350 Connecticut Avenue, NW, Suite 405,
Washington, DC 20036
Phone: 202-466-6888 / Fax: 202-466-4918
http://www.nationalbcc.org

National Center Directory of
American Indian-Owned Businesses
National Center for American Indian Enterprise
Development National Center Headquarters
953 East Juanita Avenue, Mesa, Arizona 85204
Phone: 480-545-1298 / Fax: 480-545-4208
http://www.ncaied.org

National Center for American Indian Enterprise Dev.
953 East Juanita Avenue, Mesa, Arizona 85204
Phone: 480-545-1298 / Fax: 480-545-4208
http://www.ncaied.org

National Congress of American Indians
1301 Connecticut Ave, NW, Suite 200,
Washington, D.C. 20036
Phone: 202-466-7767 / Fax: 202-466-7797
http://www.ncai.org

National Council of La Raza (NCLR)
Raul Yzaguirre Building
1126 16th Street, NW, Washington, DC 20036
Phone: 202-785-1670 / Fax: 202-776-1792
http://www.nclr.org

National Indian Gaming Association
224 Second Street SE, Washington, DC 20003
Phone: 202-546-7711 / Fax: 202-546-1755
http://www.indiangaming.org

National Latina Business Women Association
Phone: 1 888 MY-NLBWA
http://www.nlbwa.org

National Minority Business Council Inc.
120 Broadway, 19th Floor, New York, NY 10271
Phone: 212-693-5050 / Fax: 212-693-5048
http://www.nmbc.org

National Minority Supplier Development Council, Inc. (NMSDC)
1359 Broadway, 10th Floor, New York, NY 10018
Phone: 212-944-2430, ext. 124 / Fax: 212-719-9611
http://www.nmsdcus.org

National Urban League
120 Wall Street, New York, NY 10005
Phone: 212-558-5300 / Fax: 212-344-5332
http://nul.org

National Venture Capital Association
1655 North Fort Myer Drive Suite 850
Arlington, VA 22209
Phone: 703-524-2549 / Fax: 703-524-3940
http://www.nvca.org

S.C.O.R.E. (Service Core of Retired Executives)
740 15th Street, N.W.American Bar Association Building
Washington, DC 20005
Phone: (202) 272-0390
http://www.score.org

U.S.-ASEAN Business Council
1101 17th Street, NW, Suite 411, Washington, DC 20036
Phone: 202-289-1911 / Fax: 202-289-0519
http://www.us-asean.org

U.S. Hispanic Chamber of Commerce
1424 K Street, NW, Suite 401, Washington, DC 20005
Phone: 202-842-1212 / Toll-free: 1-800-874-2286
Fax: 202-842-3221
http://www.ushcc.com

U.S. Pan Asian American Chamber of Commerce
1329 19th Street, NW, Washington, DC 20036
Phone: 202-296-5221 / Toll-free: 1-800-696-7818
Fax: 202-296-5225
http://www.uspaacc.com

Women's Business Enterprise National Council (WBENC)
1120 Connecticut Avenue, NW, Suite 1000,
Washington, DC 20036
Phone: 202-872-5515 / Fax: 202-872-5505
http://www.wbenc.org

GOVERNMENT WEB SITES YOU SHOULD KNOW

The Web sites listed below are provided to help you gain access to information, contracting opportunities and much more.

- Acquisition – www.acquisition.gov

- Americans with Disabilities - www.disabilityinfo.gov

- Business - www.business.gov

- Central Contractor Registration – www.ccr.gov

- Consumer Financial Protection Bureau – www.consumerfinance.gov

- Equal Employment Opportunity Commission – www.eeoc.gov

- Expect more from your government – www.expectmore.gov

- Export-Import Bank the United States – www.exim.gov

- Federal Business Opportunities – www.fbo.gov

- Federal Deposit Insurance Corporation – http://www.fdic.gov/

- Federal Trade Commission – www.ftc.gov

- General Services Administration – www.gsa.gov

- Government Loans – www.govloans.gov

- Grants – www.grants.gov

- Internal Revenue Service – www.irs.gov

- Minority Business Development Agency – www.mbda.gov

- National Do Not Call Registry – www.donotcall.gov

- Protect your company – www.ready.gov

- Recalls: online resources for recalls – www.recalls.gov

- Senate Committee on Small Business and Entrepreneurship – www.sbc.senate.gov

- Small Business Administration – www.sba.gov

- SBA's Office of the National Ombudsman www.sba.gov.ombudsman

- SBA's Office of Advocacy www.sba.gov/advo

- Small Business Fraud Alerts – www.ftc.gov/bcp/menu-fran.htm

- System for Awards Management – www.sam.gov

- US Federal Acquisition Regulations – www.arnet.gov/far

- Veterans in Business – www.vetbiz.gov

- Veteran's Entrepreneurial Guide – www.veteranscorp.gov

- US Securities and Exchange Commission – www.sec.gov

- US Citizens and Immigration Services – www.uscis.gov

- US Patent and Trade Office – www.uspto.gov

- US Government made easy – www.usa.gov

- US Government Access – www.gpoaccess.gov

- US Food and Drug Administration – www.fda.gov

DIRECTORIES

- US Census Bureau – www.census.gov

- US Government Spending – www.usaspending.gov

- US Dept of Labor – www.dol.gov

- US Bureau of Labor and Statistics – www.bls.gov

- US Bureau of Economic Analysis – www.bea.gov

- Women Business Owners – www.womenbiz.gov

  www.women-21.gov

  www.onlinewbc.gov

BUSINESS & FINANCIAL
GLOSSARY

A

Account Creditor: Another name for the client

Account Debtor: Refers to another name for the client's customers; the entity that the factoring funder collects from

Accounts Payable: Money the client pays out or owes

Accounts Receivable: Money received or owed to the client

Accounts Receivable Financ-ing: A financing method using a company's current accounts receivable in a pool as collateral in obtaining necessary financing and is based on volume and strength of the company seeking this type of financing.

Advance Rate: The percentage of money that a factor advances its clients upon the sale of its invoices.

Angel Investor: A private individual or business associate within a local region who invests in local or regional businesses and usually does not require the same strict guidelines as the banks or management involvement the way a venture capitalist would

Asset Based: A business loan where the borrower pledges as collateral for the loan any assets used in the conduct of his or her business. Funds are used for business-related expenses. All asset-based loans are secured.

Assignment: The transfer of rights, title, interest, and benefits of a contract or financial instrument to a third party

Automated Clearing House (ACH): A secure payment transfer system that connects all US financial institutions. The ACH network acts as the central clearing facility for all electronic fund transfer transactions that occur nationwide, representing a crucial link in the national banking system.

B

"B" through "D" credit customers: Refers to consumers who have less-than-perfect to bad credit. In most instances, they cannot qualify for traditional financing. They are also called sub-prime credit customers.

Bad Debt: Any debt that is

delinquent and has been written off as uncollectible

Bad Debt Reserve: A reserve of funds held back by a factor when purchasing invoices to offset its losses in the event of non-payment. Once the reserve reaches a predetermined size sufficient to protect the funding source's investment, part of the reserve is rebated to the client.

Balance sheet: A financial statement that shows a business's current financial condition, with assets on the left side and liabilities and net worth on the right side

Balloon Payment: The balance of principal that is due and owing in its entirety at a specified time, but in any event, less than the time required to fully amortize the debt

Bankruptcy: A state of insolvency of an individual or organization, due to their inability to pay debts, for which bankruptcy protects them from creditors.

Beneficiary: The person or party entitled to receive the benefits, or proceeds, of a life insurance policy upon the death of the insured person.

Bill of Lading: A shipping document that gives instructions to the company transporting the goods

Bill of Sale: A document used in the title transfer for certain goods from seller to buyer

Broker: A company or person who arranges, for a fee, transactions between clients seeking financing and funding sources with the financial assets and expertise in their given area to finance the prospective client. Brokers can be found in many industries, including commercial and residential real estate, factoring, and equipment leasing.

C

Closed-end lease: A true lease in which the lessor assumes the depreciation risk. The lessee bears no obligation at the end of the lease but does not have the option to purchase.

Concentration: The part of the client's accounts receivable due from a single customer that is more than 50% of the client's total accounts receivable.

Credit Card Advance: A cash advance on a business's future credit card sales.

Credit Rating: A predictor of the ability to pay back a loan. The credit rating is a result of credit scoring

Credit Report: A consumer or business financial history report supplied by a credit reporting firm like Equifax, Experian, TransUnion, or Dun & Bradstreet. This report contains credit information on a business or individual, including payment history on credit cards, student loans and mortgages, and any applicable negative reporting by firms with which the business or consumer might have issues.

Credit Scoring: The reporting system used by lenders in determining the creditworthiness of a business or consumer. The lender generally considers such factors as credit payment history, inquiry history, financial strength and longevity of business.

goods, requiring an assurance of payment.

Deferred Payment Lease: A payment schedule that allows you to defer your first payment by 60 or 90 days.

Discount Fee: The fee that the factor charges when purchasing an invoice.

Dollar Buyout: Assuming that the lessee is not in default, a dollar buyout is an option at the end of the lease to buy the leased property for $1.00.

Dun & Bradstreet: D&B is the leading provider of business credit information. All companies, especially those wanting to contract with government agencies must get the identification number provided by this company.

D

E

Debt Financing: A loan with pre-agreed terms, including payback schedule and interest

Deed of Assignment: A banking arrangement between the beneficiary of a letter of credit and a third party, usually the supplier of the

Effective Lease Rate: The effective lease rate to the lessee of cash flows in a lease transaction.

Equifax: One of the three leading providers of personal credit information.

Equipment Leases: Leases allowing companies to purchase new equipment.

Exit Strategy: An intended method of getting out of a financing obligation, such as the sale of the company to receive the amount of monetary investment with interest.

Experian: One of three leading providers of personal and business credit information

F

Factoring: The process where you sell your current accounts receivable at a discount. This type of alternative financing has been heavily used in industries such as the manufacturing, garment, and staffing industries.

Factor's Acknowledgment Form: A form sent to the client's customer by the factor, confirming that the client's invoice is genuine and that the customer will remit the payment due under that invoice to the factor

Factor's Advance: The money the factor sends to the client up front, after the verification process is complete, and before the factor receives its money from the client's customer. The advance is figured as a percentage of the face value of the factored invoices.

Factor's Charge-Back: An amount of money owed to the factor and deducted or charged back from the reserve or availability of the line based on an agreed-upon non-payment by debtor clause in the factor's contract.

Factors Fee: The fee the factor charges for funding the client's receivables.

Factors Reserve: The money retained by the factor when the advance is sent to the client. The reserve is then sent to the client after the customer has paid the factor the money due on the invoice.

Factor's Reserve Release: The amount of money released from the factor's reserve once payment has been received and credited. If there are any charge- backs or fees associated with the services, the reserve release will be less.

Factor's Verification: The process by which the factor verifies that the product or service provided by the client was received and accepted by the customer and that the customer intends to pay the factor the payable amount due. This process takes place before the factor sends the advance funds to the client.

Fictitious Name: A legal statement filed when a person uses a name other than his or her own to operate an unincorporated business.

Fair Market Value Purchase Option: An end-of-term lease option that allows a lessor to purchase the equipment at its fair market value

Finance Lease: A type of lease that gives the option to purchase the equipment for a nominal fee at the end of the lease

FICO: The Fair Isaac Corpor-ation credit reporting system was developed by engineer Bill Fair and mathematician Earl Isaac. FICO determines a credit score using variables that identify a lender's risk level when extending credit to an individual.

Friends and Relatives: You, like most of us, are probably reluctant to ask friends and relatives for money, but many people do, at one stage or another, when they are running their own businesses.

Fixed Interest Rate: An interest rate that is the same throughout the life of a loan

H

Hypothecate: A form of moving an asset or any negotiable instrument from a position of priority lien to a lesser position to secure additional financing.

I

Income Stream: A series of payments over a period of time or amount of cash to be received from an investment or other business or personal transaction.

Interest Rate: The percentage amount charged by a lender for the money borrowed.

Inventory Financing: Money borrowed against finished goods. The loan is paid as inventory is sold.

Invoice Factoring: The sale of an invoice for immediate cash.

L

Lease Financing: A financing option

used when a business owner is seeking to purchase equipment such as vehicles, machinery, office furniture, software, and any other type of products that a lease financing company will finance.

Lessee: The party that leases equipment for its own use.

Lessor: The party to a lease agreement that has legal or tax title to the equipment for the lease term and is entitled to the rental fees.

Letter of Credit: A bank commitment on behalf of a client to pay a beneficiary a stated amount of money under specified conditions.

Leveraged Lease: In this type of lease, the lessor provides an equity portion (usually 20 to 40 percent) of the equipment cost, and lenders provide the balance on a non-recourse debt basis. The lessor receives the tax benefits of ownership.

Line of Credit: Access to a set amount of money that a business can borrow against at times it needs capital.

Loan Term: The length of time in months and years that the borrower has to repay loan.

Long-Term Debt: Financing used to purchase or improve company assets such as manufacturing plants, facilities, large equipment, and real estate.

M

Master Lease: A contract wherein the lessee leases currently needed assets and is able to acquire other assets under the same basic terms and conditions without negotiating a new contract.

Maturity: A loan's maturity is the number of months or years of the loan; that is, how long you have to repay the loan. It primarily applies to term loans.

Merchant Category Code (MCC): A four-digit number assigned by MasterCard or Visa to identify card users by categories. It tracks and restricts certain purchases.

N

Net Lease: A lease where payments to the lessor do not include insurance and maintenance. They are paid separately by the lessee.

Non-Payout Lease: A lease in which the cash flows will not be sufficient to cover the full costs of the equipment, the costs of financing and the costs of administration. To provide a satisfactory return and profit, the lessor looks to the residual.

Non-Recourse Factoring: Factoring where the funding source purchases receivables and assumes full credit risk for non-payment by a customer.

Notification: A characteristic of factoring whereby the factor takes assignment of the accounts receivable and notifies the customers of the client to pay the factor directly.

O

Open-End Lease: A lease that includes a provision for extending payments under the lease on predetermined terms after a set period of time

Operating Lease: One of the two major types of equipment leases (the other type is a capital lease). An operating lease is a contract that requires the lessee (the party that uses the equipment) to make periodic payments to the lessor

(the party that retains ownership of the equipment) over the length of the lease term.

P

Paydex Score: A credit score for businesses through Dun & Bradstreet

Personal Guarantee: A guarantee of payment that the primary owner of the company signs off on when obtaining a loan.

Personal Loans: Loans made to individuals with good credit standing.

Platinum Lease: A lease structure that allows you to add new equipment on an ongoing basis without changing the basic terms or conditions.

Present Value: Calculates the current value of a future expected payment. The present value of any future payments would be calculated at a discount such as a "discounted cash value".

Private Equity: Refers to equity position investment in a nonpublic company.

Prime Rate: A rate the lender

charges its best customers. This rate is calculated differently by each lender.

Purchase Order: An order submitted to a company to provide the commercial purchaser source with the requested product order based on specific terms and conditions.

Purchase Order Financing: Short-term financing method to allow a corporation to purchase raw materials or finished goods quickly.

R

Reserve: In Factoring, this refers to the percent advanced, minus the factor's discount fee.

Revolving Credit: An amount of money a business owner can borrow against when needing working capital. It is similar to a line of credit that can be accessed by check, ATM or business credit or debit card.

S

Sale-Leaseback: An arrangement whereby equipment is purchased by a lessor from the company owning and using it. The lessor then becomes the owner and leases it back to the original owner, who continues to use the equipment.

SBA Loan: A loan made to a small business that is unable to secure financing on reasonable terms through normal lending institutions. The SBA does not provide financing directly but through its Loan Guarantee programs. The SBA uses private sector lenders who provide these loans.

Secured Loan: A loan secured by specific collateral. This loan could be secured with real estate, inventory, accounts receivable, machinery and/or other equipment.

Seed Money: The first round of capital investment from a venture capital firm to a start-up business.

Small Business Administra-tion (SBA): A government agency that provides financial, technical, and management assistance to help businesses start, run and grow.

Short-Term Debt: Financing used to secure cash for accounts payable and inventory

Subordination: The act of a creditor acknowledging in writing that they are willing to take a secondary position on debt due by a debtor. The creditor in second position is willing to do so in order to facilitate the successful completion of a particular transaction.

T

Tax Lease: A lease wherein the lessor recognizes the tax incentives provided by the tax laws for investment and ownership of equipment. Generally, the lease rate factor on tax leases is reduced to reflect the lessor's recognition of this tax incentive.

Term Loan: A loan for a specific amount of money that has either a fixed or variable interest rate with a set payment schedule. These loans mature usually in one to fifteen years.

Time Value of Money: The concept of money being available today is worth more now than in the future due to the current money's potential earning powers. Use interchangeable with *"Present Value"*.

TRAC Lease: A tax-oriented lease of motor vehicles or trailers that contains a terminal rental adjustment clause and otherwise complies with the requirements of the tax laws.

TransUnion Corporation: One of the three leading providers of personal credit information.

True Lease: A transaction that qualifies as a lease under the Internal Revenue Code. It allows the lessor to claim ownership and the lessee to claim rental payment as tax deductions.

Truth in Lending: A federal law requiring disclosure of the annual percentage rate to home buyers shortly after they apply for the loan.

U

Uniform Commercial Code (UCC): A law that regulates the transfer of personal property. It is also a statutory law covering most commercial transactions.

UCC-1 (Uniform Commercial Code-1 Financial Form) This is the legal document a creditor files with the applicable Secretary of State office stating interest in a particular individual or company's assets as detailed in the document pursuant to a prior agreement. This serves as notice and protection for the creditor, by placing them in first position against the asset.

Unsecured Loan: A loan granted based on the good credit of the borrower with no collateral involved.

Verification: The method in which a factoring source validates invoices they purchase by communicating with the payer of the invoice to verify that the goods or services were in fact, provided.

V

Variable Interest Rate: An interest rate that changes during the lifetime of the loan.

Vendor Leasing: A working relationship between a financing source and a vendor to provide financing to stimulate the vendor's sales. The financing source offers leases or conditional sales contracts to the vendor's customers.

Venture Capital: A private investment of money, time, and/or personnel into a client's company. Venture capitalists do not finance many companies, as they are very selective in the type of companies they finance. Despite all the attention venture capital firms get in the business press, they actually finance very few businesses. The better venture capital firms are deluged with proposals from budding entrepreneurs, but most entrepreneurial proposals are inappropriate to the goals of venture capitalists.

Y

Yield: The rate of return on an investment using such factors as annual interest payments, purchase price and the time remaining until maturity.

ABOUT THE AUTHOR

Karlene Sinclair-Robinson is an entrepreneur. However, this does not truly define her. She is a teacher at heart! When there are problems, she finds solutions, and that is Karlene's mantra. She felt breaking into the entrepreneurial world would seem like a breeze. However, Karlene soon discovered that none of her previous work-life experiences could truly have prepared her for this journey. She started out over 10 years ago and failed at her first 2 start-ups.

With a background in business management, home healthcare and financing, Karlene spent several years working with small business owners and witnessed their inability to access capital through traditional banks. Nearly all of these struggling business owners were not aware of alternative financing solutions, nor did they understand them, even if they were.

Karlene realized that there was a need for Non-Traditional Banking or Alternative Financing Solutions for businesses that could not qualify through institutional sources. The key is to find a solution to the entrepreneur's need, implement it and provide proven benefits of said solution. She decided to fill the void by writing this book.

Karlene's decision to publish *Spank the Bank; THE Guide to Alternative Business Financing* stemmed from a variety of factors. The innumerable list exposed the following failures: the inability, inexperience, lack of knowledge and failure of business owners, lending institutions with the "Looking Back" mentality, and finally, the government who all played a role in the puzzle that made up our economic meltdown. We must fix it.

Karlene is the Managing Member of KsR Solutions LLC, a business consulting firm focused on strategic business solutions, including financing and diversification. She has been successful in assisting numerous clients in accessing millions of dollars through non-traditional financing, even those with less-than-stellar credit. In addition, she teaches entrepreneurship and alternative financing at local small business development centers and community colleges in Northern Virginia and Maryland.

Karlene is married with two children, a son diagnosed with autism and a daughter. She resides in Northern Virginia with her family.

If you would like to connect with Karlene, you may contact her via info@SpankTheBank.biz or follow her on Twitter at @ KarleneSinRob.

Media Contact:
Barry Cohen
AdLab Media Communications
barry@adlabcreative.com
www.adlabcreative.com

CPSIA information can be obtained
at www.ICGtesting.com
Printed in the USA
BVOW11s1349240316
441451BV00008B/257/P